SUPERHUMAN MEMORY

The Comprehensive Guide To Increase Your Memory, Learning Abilities, And Speed Reading By 500% - Develop A Photographic Memory

© Copyright 2017 by Keith Hope_- All rights reserved.

This document is geared towards providing exact and reliable information in regards to the topic and issue covered. The publication is sold on the idea that the publisher is not required to render an accounting service, officially permitted, or otherwise, qualified services. If advice is necessary, legal or professional, a practiced individual in the profession should be consulted.

- From a Declaration of Principles which was accepted and approved equally by a Committee of the American Bar Association and a Committee of Publishers and Associations.

In no way is it legal to reproduce, duplicate, or transmit any part of this document by either electronic means or in printed format. Recording of this publication is strictly prohibited, and any storage of this material is not allowed unless with written permission from the publisher. All rights reserved.

The information provided herein is stated to be truthful and consistent, in that any liability, regarding inattention or otherwise, by any usage or abuse of any policies, processes, or directions contained within is the sole and utter responsibility of the recipient reader. Under no circumstances will any legal liability or blame be held against the publisher for any reparation, damages, or monetary loss due to the information herein, either directly or indirectly.

Respective authors own all copyrights not held by the publisher.

The information herein is offered for informational purposes solely and is universal as so. The presentation of the information is without a contract or any guarantee assurance.

The trademarks that are used are without any consent, and the publication of the trademark is without permission or backing by the trademark owner. All trademarks and brands within this book are for clarifying purposes only and are the owned by the owners themselves, not affiliated with this document.

Thank you for purchasing

SUPERHUMAN MEMORY

Contents

Introduction 1

Chapter 1: Why bother when you can Google? 5

Chapter 2: Time Management - Tomato Time 12

Chapter 3: Uses of Memory Hacks 17

Chapter 4: The Magical World of Mnemonics 23

Chapter 5: The Peg or Rhyme System 33

Chapter 6: The Major System 46

Chapter 7: Creating Effective Passwords 64

Chapter 8: Practice with Mind Maps 67

Chapter 9: Major System Imagery 72

Chapter 10: Memory Palace or
Loci Method to Remember digits of Pi 125

Chapter 11: Driving Directions and The Major System ... 142

Chapter 12: Remembering License Plates 146

Chapter 13: Memorize a Deck of Cards:
Major System Practice 149

Chapter 14: Memorize the US Presidents 161

Chapter 15: Periodic Table Mnemonics:
Major System Practice 169

Chapter 16: Geological Formations 183

Chapter 17: Brain Hacks to Remember 187

Bibliography 200

Endnotes 204

"Every human being is a Leonardo da Vinci. The only problem is that he doesn't know it. His parents didn't know it, and they didn't treat him like a Leonardo. Therefore he didn't become like a Leonardo.
That's my basic theory."

Öystein Skalleberk[i]

Introduction

Memory is a skill, which means it is something you can learn. It is something you can constantly improve upon. You have the ability, given the right tools, to achieve memory feats beyond your wildest imagination.

A couple of years ago I set out on my memory journey. I took a finance seminar, where a certification required that I memorize seemingly endless and incredibly boring dates and legal sections.

In order to procrastinate, and figure out a way to make something incredibly boring interesting, I started reading articles on memory and then completely changed my career path.

I was only looking for better ways to remember dates and codes that were meaningless to be but stumbled upon a treasure trove of information and knowledge dating back to the ancient Greeks.

Memory does not just come in handy when memorizing less than exciting material for work and school.

I spend most of my time traveling around the world and consider myself a true digital nomad. However, all this comes with a number of downsides.

Over the years, I have gotten myself into a number of hairy situations.

Some years ago, I was traveling to Spain, where I was to be staying with a host, whose address I was given by an agency. I landed in Madrid in the pouring rain with four massive suitcases.

The address I was given was wrong, the cab driver didn't speak English and I didn't speak a whole lot of Spanish. My phone didn't work. There was no cell or data reception.

I couldn't remember the number of the agent and lost the paperwork during the commotion.

I ended up standing on a street corner, soaking wet, jetlagged, unable to move with all of my luggage, in front of a shut gate in a residential area with no foot traffic in the pouring rain.

It ended well, but quick recall of an important number would have saved me a lot of frustration and headache.

Being a single female traveler at the time, I have encountered a number of situations where it was paramount that I know all the emergency phone numbers upon landing in a country.

After a particularly frightening encounter with a driver of a shuttle service abroad, I got into the habit of always memorizing the license plate number of any car I get into as well as the roads/highways I am to be traveling on.

What this program aims to accomplish is incredible feats of memory where you can see the results right away so there is no doubt that it works. I have read time and time again that memory champions are just ordinary people with ordinary IQs. If they can do it, then so can you.

I started reading fascinating accounts of memory champions. Unfortunately, they did not go into as much detail as I would have liked on how they managed to achieve such feats. There were descriptions of generic techniques, but without step-by-step instructions as well as ready imagery, one quickly lost interest.

Study after study has shown that memory champions are not natural born geniuses. They just train their brains to remember better.

I am no genius and I do not participate in memory championships, but I do remember car rental license plates from a year ago, my credit and debit cards, my passport number, and my driver's license number along with a host of other important details.

The history of humanity is lined with stories of extraordinary accomplishments of genius for some, however, for the masses, sadly it is a story of limitations.

Whenever you embark on learning a new skill, one that is not something that mainstream education promotes, you are likely to meet with skepticism.

This course is just one of many ways to enhance your extraordinary built in gifts in a supercomputer called the human brain.

Since you have picked up this product, I have to assume that you believe that you do not have a worldview filled with limitations. You believe that there is so much more out there that you could master or do better.

No matter your current age or education level, you can get better and better at memorization using these techniques as long as you are able to read and understand this program. School is not the end all be all of education. One should never stop learning and memory is a building block of all knowledge. You have to remember the basics in order to build on it and become an expert in any subject.

Our brains encode and retain information much more efficiently when we store the information in a memorable way, even if it seems silly.

The more colorful, outrageous or even violent the image, the more it will stand out as extraordinary information, and the easier it will be to recall.

Reading books about memory will familiarize you with the numerous methods, which in turn you will intellectualize but will not necessarily be able to practice.

I first found use for remembering contract paragraphs while working as an executive in business process outsourcing. Most people don't read contracts, unless they are the assigned to the project.

Most people skim contracts, but they are not able to quote paragraphs and page numbers, on which there is critical information.

I wish I had discovered a similar product many years ago during the freshman year of college, or even in high school. It would have made a great deal of difference to my academic performance, even my standardized test scores, however, as many other skills, this is one that will benefit you for life.

You do need to put in effort, it takes more than just reading through the books. You need to follow through and do the exercises and start applying the techniques in every day life. If you do, the rewards will be beyond your wildest imagination.

Chapter 1:
Why bother when you can Google?

I'm sure you thought at least once about why you should bother with memory when you can just type whatever you need at an instant into a search engine. Well, there are plenty of good reasons why.

Most of us know how to use the Internet. When you are hired for a job, Internet use in this day and age is a basic assumed skill but I don't know anyone who was hired for their ability to Google or type a query into any other search engine.

Can you have an intelligent political/economic/historical discussion without previously having retained information?

Can you have a debate or presentation of any kind without being prepared with information/facts?

The answer is no, you cannot. You need to have a certain amount of built up knowledge base to debate anyone.

Technically, for a public speaking engagement, you could have a teleprompter or low-tech note cards, but in order to be really convincing, you need to remember your talking points and worry about what comes next while you are still speaking.

When you are in a meeting or part of a negotiation, the speed of recall without having to look it up on your smartphone is an indicator of knowledge and intelligence. Being able to quote facts and figures on the spot is not only impressive, it sets you apart from everyone else.

Think of memory as a foundation for all new learning. Everything we learn is based on the solid foundation of things we already know. Without memory, learning is pointless as you can't retain anything you have learned. Knowledge is built on already existing building blocks.

IMPORTANT: While you will learn a fair amount just by reading this book, you actually have to sit down and do the exercises for it to have any long-term effect. All it takes is 25 minutes per day over a 30-day period after reading the book to gain fantastic results. It's like learning a foreign language, just much faster. You are training your brain to process and store information in a different way.

The key is practice. Being able to effectively use mnemonics and convert numbers and lists into imagery is a life-long skill. Much like learning how to type on a keyboard, drive a car or being able to play a musical instrument. It takes less time than mastering any of the above tasks, yet it is incredibly rewarding.

Expectations

While you can benefit very quickly from the Memory Palace or Method of Loci as well as the Remember Faces Module, a fair amount of effort is required of you in mastering the Major System.

This may seem excessive at first, in our culture of instant gratification, however, once mastered, this system is incredibly powerful.

If you find learning the major system images, you can slow down and spend as little as 5 minutes a day on them. You will master the system in a relatively short time and you will speak the language of mnemonics.

Think of how your life would be different if you mastered these techniques in this system. What new skills would you use it to learn? How would it help you in your everyday life?

"The world as we have created, it is a process of our thinking. It cannot be changed without changing our thinking."

— ***Albert Einstein***

How to Complete this Program

Memory Mastery Instructions

25 minutes/day
30 days

Once you get to the Major System Chapters (Chapters 6-9) in this book – you should spend a minimum of 5 minutes/day on practicing them.

In no time, the techniques in this book will become second nature, just like typing or driving.

Even if you have heard of the Major System before and understand how it works, there is a great deal of difference between understanding on an intellectual level vs. mastery and every day application to your life.

Remember, the key to hacking superhuman memory is creativity!

"Creativity is intelligence having fun."

Albert Einstein

"You can't use up creativity. The more you use, the more you have."

Maya Angelou

Chapter 2:
Time Management - Tomato Time

In order to master the art of memory conversion, you should spend 25 minutes per day for 30 days on completing this program for intermediate mastery.

It's very easy to get distracted with checking social media/emails, the news and many other minor distractions. When I set the timer, I only focus on the task at hand. I close unnecessary browsers and put my phone on silent.

On average, it takes about 21 days to develop a new habit. For advanced mastery, complete the advanced workbook over the course of 60 days.

I recommend reading through the book first, then, cut out the memory cards and commence the daily exercises in the Major System Chapter.

In addition to each daily prescribed exercise, you will also memorize a number of items memorable to you, then practice them in the coming days.

A time management method I often use is called the Pomodoro Technique®[ii], a time management method that was invented by Francesco Cirillo in the late 1980s.

Pomodoro means "tomato" in Italian. The method was named after the tomato shaped kitchen timer that Cirillo used as a college student.

The Pomodoro Technique® breaks down tasks into 25 minute intervals, followed by short breaks. This improves flow and focus. If you are looking at longer tasks or just aiming at getting through a day at work in the most productive manner possible, I highly recommend this method.

In the Pomodoro Technique®, you take 3-5 minute breaks after each Pomodoro, or 25 minute work interval.

Four Pomodoros make up one set. After each set, one takes a 15-30 minute break. If interrupted, schedule a quick call back, make note of the distraction, and then continue the Pomodoro.

If the interruption cannot be avoided or dealt with quickly, deal with it, then restart the Pomodoro from the beginning.

Memory mastery is a lifelong process. You will find ways to create memorable images specific to you. This is a memory mastery kit to get you started on your memory journey.

This course was completed using the simple but brilliant Pomodoro Technique®, a brilliant method to overcome procrastination as well as a measurement of progress.

To this day, I measure my daily productivity on my calendar with the amount of Pomodoros I've accomplished. 🍅🍅🍅🍅 🍅🍅🍅🍅🍅🍅🍅🍅🍅🍅🍅 🍅🍅🍅 to 22 pomodoros (tomatoes) of 25 min intense work intervals = 550 minutes = 9.16 hours = 9 hours and 10 minutes of pure productivity.

"Don't say you don't have enough time. You have exactly the same number of hours per day that were given to Helen Keller, Pasteur, Michelangelo, Mother Teresa, Leonardo da Vinci, Thomas Jefferson, and Albert Einstein."

— H. Jackson Brown Jr.

Flow

I find that just setting the timer, formalizes the task and puts me in a psychological state of "Flow". Flow, a highly focused mental state is a term coined by American-Hungarian Psychologist, Mihály Csíkszentmihályi, also known for his contributions to Positive Psychology[iii].

Another expression for "Flow" is being in the zone. Once you are in the zone, time ceases, and you are at your most productive and in many ways, the happiest.

You may ask, what does a memory course have to do with positive psychology and happiness? A lot! This memory course will open up many other possibilities for you. You will see learning in a different light.

You will feel empowered at what your mind can achieve and my hope for you is that this will put you on a lifelong path to learning, not matter your chronological age or background.

" Contrary to what we usually believe, moments like these, the best moments in our lives, are not the passive, receptive, relaxing times – although such experiences can also be enjoyable, if we have worked hard to attain them.

The best moments usually occur when a person's body or mind is stretched to its limits in a voluntary effort to accomplish something difficult and worthwhile.

Optimal experience is thus something that we make happen. For a child, it could be placing with trembling fingers the last block on a tower she has built, higher than any she has built so far; for a swimmer, it could be trying to beat his own record; for a violinist, mastering an intricate musical passage.

For each person there are thousands of opportunities, challenges to expand ourselves."

- Mihaly Csikszentmihalyi, Flow: The Psychology of Optimal Experiences

Chapter 3:
Uses of Memory Hacks

What can you use this method for? Why bother when you can just take a photo with your smartphone, write something down in your notebook, save a file on your laptop?

The implications are potentially endless, but here are a few:

- ID, Cards, Finances
- Remember crucial details such as account numbers and personal ID numbers for you and your family members.
- Contract clauses and important page numbers
- Recall names of people you meet
- Lists such as grocery lists
- Help your kids learn historic dates for school
- Impress your friends, family, colleagues
- Get a head start to enter memory competitions
- Prompt yourself while giving presentations or speeches without the need for notes

BUILDING RELATIONSHIPS

- Remember people's names
- Remember important details people tell you and in turn gain their trust and possibly their business

Safety

- Remember the license plates of cabs you get into at a glance. Who knows if you'll need to call for help while inside someone else's car.

- Immediately recall ID, credit and billing information in case of loss or theft.
- Remember passwords to numerous accounts such as email accounts, subscriptions, online bank/loan accounts.

Travel

- Remember flight numbers and times
- Remember rental car and taxi license plates
- Immediately recall ID, credit and billing information in case of loss or theft.
- Learn local emergency numbers in seconds.
- Breeze through a survival course in a local language by quickly remembering key phrases.
- Remember driving directions

Academics/News Skills

- Retain much more information from classes you take or books/articles you read
- Recall recipes/ingredient lists and quantities
- Teach your kids, colleagues, significant other to improve their memory
- Become a more efficient debater by being able to recall relevant facts faster
- Enhance your knowledge of art history – knowing the era a painter was active during, can immediately tie him to his artist peers thereby enhancing your gallery experience or dazzle your new date.
- Impress people with your knowledge of historical events.

Workplace & Business

- Be more persuasive by recalling facts and relevant information on the spot
- Increased efficiency when referring to paragraphs and important page numbers in contracts and other crucial documentation
- Recall commitments
- Remember names of customer service reps who committed to carrying out tasks for you with ease.
- Setting complex passwords and remembering them with ease.

Learning Styles

Before we go in depth into the many fascinating learning methods, I'd like to take a look at the VAK/VARK learning styles developed by William Bare in 1981, later expanded by Neil Flemming[iv].

Understanding your learning style can help you adapt your study strategies. It is also very helpful if you have children as you can give them an advantage by adapting the way they absorb information.

Visual: A person with a visual learning style responds well to visual aids such as images, charts/flowcharts, vectors, power-point type presentations and graphs.

Someone who forms mental images, especially from abstract concepts will be responsive to this learning style.

Aural: A person with an aural learning style uses hearing and speech to encode information. They may need to say words aloud or mentally to be able to process the information.

They may often mention that they need to "talk things through".

Read/Write: The basis for encoding is textual, which means that the person has to write or type the information. People tend to be fond of lists, dictionaries like Wikipedia as well as presentation slides.

Kinesthetic: The person learns by doing, by trial and error, tactically. What is being learned should be related to something "real" that can be touched or experienced directly.

instead of an abstract idea, they respond well to case studies or video examples based on reality.

If you think you fall into more than one category, don't worry. It is possible to have a mix of learning styles.

The Three-Step Process of Memorization

When we need to memorize something, we go through a three-step process.

1. ENCODING
2. STORAGE (Short-Term or Long-Term)
3. RETRIEVAL

Encoding is finding a way to effectively store the information in your brain.

Storage is either Short-Term or Long-Term memory. As the definition states, short-term memory has limited capacity and holds information for a very short time and long-term memory stores information (quite a lot at that) pretty much indefinitely.

The more you repeat information, the more it is likely to be stored in long-term memory. Long-term memory is fairly passive in nature.

Depending on the information, it stays there for a very long time. Certain types of information are easier to store than others.

In the Memory Palace chapter, you will learn about being a born geospatial genius. Once you have walked through a house, you are likely to remember intimate details and locations without much repetition. The more meaning something holds, the more you are likely it is to be stored away in long-term memory.

There is another type of memory called "working memory", which is not very different from short-term memory. Working memory is for getting things done such as calculations in your head and not adding the same ingredient twice, when say, baking a cake[v].

Retrieval

Even if you have encoded something for long-term memory storage, it is possible that you may need certain cues such as the first letter of the word/name of person or object to retrieve it.

Think of looking for a lost item in a messy and cluttered house versus an neatly organized house where everything is nicely folded and organized by category, seasonality, utility etc. There is a big difference between the two.

When it comes to an untrained memory, our minds are cluttered and information is difficult to retrieve.

Coincidentally, people who purchase intelligence and memory related products also tend to buy digital products and books on de-cluttering topics, without even being consciously aware of the connection.

In the Superhuman Memory System, I will only teach you techniques where you will see immediate results.

Chapter 4:
The Magical World of Mnemonics

What are mnemonics?

The dictionary definition of memonic[vi] is something that is intended to aid with memory or a technique for improving memory.

Even if you haven't heard the term "mnemonic", you probably learned a number of mnemonic techniques as early as grade school, you just didn't know the term for it.

Learning a Foreign Language

The more I get involved with mnemonics, the more amazing uses I discover. My absolute favorite foreign language mnemonic is Dr. Moku's system for learning to read and write the Japanese Hiragana and Katakana alphabets.

The images are being included with the creator Bob Byrne's permission. This is not a paid endorsement; we are just massive fans of Dr. Moku[vii] !

You can learn the Japanese Hiragana or Katakana alphabets in an hour. It's fun and you will feel brilliant once you do. I wasn't even planning on learning Japanese until I stumbled upon this app.

You can check it out on Drmoku.com or download the app. The combination of imagination, graphics and humor, such key characteristics of mnemonics, will have you reading/writing Japanese in no time, even if you do not particularly excel when it comes to foreign languages.

This system further proves that the key to remembering is creativity and imagination, not pure just repetition.

I have enclosed a few examples of the app for leaning Hiragana, the basic Japanese phonetic alphabet, representing sounds in the Japanese language.

Medical Mnemonics

There are so many applications of mnemonics. If you are headed off to medical school or just want to better understand when a doctor who is speaking a seemingly foreign language, there are a variety of mnemonics apps in the app store to help you remember.

Since we are dedicating this course to maximizing memory power, we should dedicate this section to parts of the brain.

Remember when I told you that you probably learned a few mnemonics in school? This is one you would have most likely learnt in science class.

If you want to remember the lobes (Frontal, Temporal, Parietal, Occipital) of the brain, use:

Freud	Tore his	Pants	Off
R	E	A	C
O	M	R	C
N	P	I	I
T	O	E	P
A	R	T	P
L	A	A	I
	L	L	T
			A
			L

The **FRONTAL LOBE** processes complex thoughts. Think of your inner genius sitting up front on your forehead.

The **TEMPORAL LOBE** processes auditory information. Picture a pianist listening to keep the tempo.

The **PARIETAL LOBE** is responsible for processing sensory information, including pain and touch. Think of a parent patting a kid on top of his head, where the parietal lobe is located.

The **OCCIPITAL LOBE** is responsible for processing visual information. Think of an octopus with huge eyes.

The **HIPPOCAMPUS** is responsible for memory. Think of a hippo who is wandering around a college campus trying to remember which class he has to go to.

The **AMYGDALA** is in charge of the fear response. Think of a scared girl named Amy.

The **CEREBELLUM** handles fine motor movement and balance. Think of someone trying to balance without ringing a bell she is carrying.

ACRONYMS

One method of learning that our education system usually makes use of at some point during our education is acronyms.

If you commit something into long-term memory, in order to retrieve it, you may need some ques. Acronyms are perfect for this.

For example, popular acronyms and acrostics, which I can still recall from my school days:

What are the names of the **Great Lakes** in the United States? This is an acrostic.

An Acrostic is a word or poem where the first letter of each word spells out a word.

It's a mnemonic device that is meant to aid retrieval; therefore you are expected to have prior knowledge of the subject.

If you went to middle school or high school in the United States, chances are you have learned one of the below.

What are the names of the Great Lakes?

HOMES:
Huron
Ontario
Michigan
Erie
Superior

Ex.: What are the colors of the rainbow?

Richard Of York Gave Battle In Vain
Another common way to remember the rainbow spectrum of colors is: ROY.G.BIV (**Red**, Orange, Yellow, **Green**, **Blue**, **Indigo & Violet**).

"Our memory is a more perfect world than the universe: it gives back life to those who no longer exist."

— Guy de Maupassant

Why didn't I learn memory techniques in school?

If it makes life so much easier, why haven't we been thought mnemonics in school?

The truth is that our educational system has not changed much since the industrial revolution when it comes to core subjects.

We have inherited a system of repletion and rote memory, oftentimes for things that we don't use, and therefore easily forget.

During the Industrial Revolution, the masses had to be educated just enough to be able to operate machinery in the newly built factories.

We are now playing catch-up but in many cases, schools are preparing students for jobs that do not even exist yet.

This is all the more reason to maximize our learning ability, as well as habits of lifetime learning. Let us not forget that memory is a building block for learning. We are continuously building on what we already know.

What if my teacher/parent/boss told me I was slow/stupid/(insert choice insult)?

What if I did poorly on my SATs/ACTs/other standardized test that is supposed to measure your potential for future success? People learn in many different ways and possess different kinds of intelligence.

If you took an IQ test and didn't score in the top 10%, it doesn't mean that you are any less able to learn or any less intelligent. Don't ever let a standardized test question your ability to achieve and contribute.

Many standardized tests focus on verbal and mathematical reasoning skills. However, in addition to verbal and mathematical reasoning skills there are other types of intelligence.

According to the American psychologist, Howard Gardener, there are 9 types of intelligence[viii]:

- Naturalist – nature smart
- Musical – sound smart
- Logical – Mathematical – number/reasoning smart
- Existential – Life smart
- Interpersonal – people smart
- Bodily-kinesthetic – body smart
- Linguistic – word smart
- Spatial – picture smart

We are going to use all our senses to make information come alive so our brains process it, the way it was meant to, the way it makes sense to you and is important to you.

Poisonous Mushrooms & Your Memory

Our brains have evolved to remember things a certain way in order to survive.

As cavemen/women, we needed to recognize the FACEs of friends and foes. We needed to recognize the COLOR of poisonous mushrooms and snakes to ensure our survival.

We needed to TASTE and ODOR in order to know if our food had gone bad and could make us sick or even kill us.

When I lived in Texas, we had a rattlesnakes living under our porch. They were not the most pleasant neighbors but I was certainly not going to take any chances evicting them from the neighborhood.

While the snakes weren't colorful, the SOUND of the rattle at the end of their tail certainly did a good job with a warning to stay away.

These are the very senses we are going to use in this program to improve your memory.

Things we didn't evolve to do include storing large amounts of arbitrary information such as remembering books, names and numbers.

We also weren't meant to sit behind a desk for endless hours the same way we didn't evolve to digest large amounts of processed foods but that is content for a different book.

The Farmer – Farmer Paradox

If you go to a party, and meet a guy named John Farmer, it won't make as strong an impression as meeting an actual farmer, where you will immediately visualize him in the field, harvesting vegetables.

"Farmer" as an occupation is much more descriptive of a person than having the last name "Farmer". Immediately a vivid mental picture comes to mind.

Having the last name "Farmer" doesn't tell you much about the person. It doesn't tell you his actual occupation, his hobbies, his work ethic etc., therefore your brain tends to ignore this arbitrary piece of information.

This is also known as the **Baker/Baker Paradox.**

We deal with remembering people's names in detail in the Superhuman Memory: Remember Names e-book.

The important point to remember here is that you always want to think in vivid pictures with ACTION.

The more of your senses (taste, smell, sight, hearing, touch) you can activate, the easier and longer your brain will remember.

You will learn to build your memory by thinking in pictures.

"You should always be taking pictures, if not with a camera then with your mind. Memories you capture on purpose are always more vivid than the ones you pick up by accident."

— ***Isaac Marion, Warm Bodies***

Chapter 5:
The Peg or Rhyme System

Remember learning nursery rhymes and songs when you were a kid? It's no coincidence that we teach young kids things that are easy to remember.

Rhyme may seem silly once you are all grown up but your brain still retains this kind of information much more efficiently.

It is still much easier to remember song lyrics, slogans and poems that rhyme than any old regular text for us "big kids".

Well, we are going to make the most of this mental gift and apply it to our memory. Let me take you step by step for this simple yet very important and useful exercise. This technique has been around a very long time. Henry Herdson is credited with its invention in the 1600's.[ix]

This exercise is usually very easy for Auditory Learners but due to its simplicity, everyone can pick it up fast.

It only requires 10 minutes on your part so please don't just read it. Practice and learn!

STEP 1

Memorize these 10 objects and attempt to repeat them in order. You have 2 minutes.

List to Memorize

1. Duck
2. Movie
3. Goat
4. Frog
5. Goggles
6. Helmet
7. Ladder
8. Robot
9. Owl
10. Golden Rock

STEP 2

How many did you get right?

Now cover up the list and answer the following question without looking at the list again.

Which object was number 3? 8? 10?

Wait and hour and see how many of the objects you can recall.

STEP 3

Now memorize the below numbers with the words that rhyme with them. This will be much easier than the previous exercise.

1. **Sun**
2. **Blue**
3. **Tree**
4. **Door**
5. **Dive**
6. **Bricks**
7. **Heaven**
8. **Date**
9. **Wine**
10. **Zen**

Once you have memorized the number rhyme pairs, go back to the original list and create a vivid image for each of the objects. In this example, we have done it for you. Check out the composite images below.

For example: One – Sun – Duck, duck being the first item you are trying to memorize while associating it with first please on the list. You can create a vivid image of a duck walking into the sunset as shown below. Do this for all of the images.

Paired Memory Images:

Number in sequence – Rhyme with Number – Item to remember

One – **Sun –** Duck	
Two – **Blue –** Movie	
Three – **Tree –** Goat	

Four-Door – Frog	
Five – Dive – Goggles	
Six-Bricks- Helmet	
Seven – Heaven – Ladder	

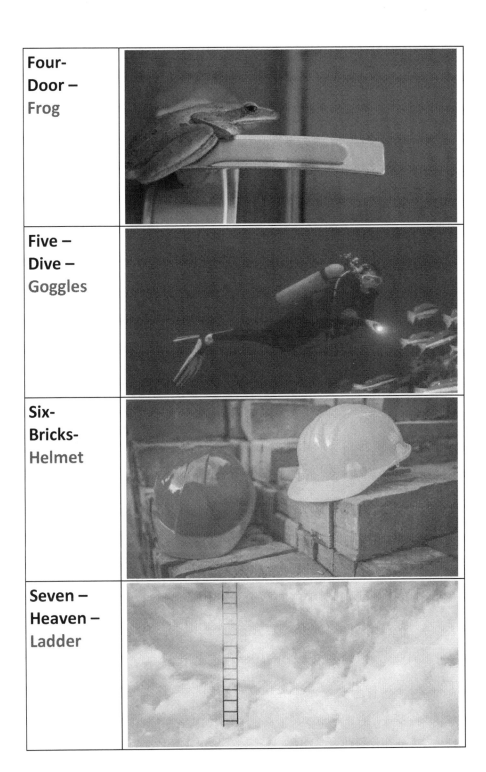

Eight – **Date –** Robot	
Nine – **Wine –** Owl	
Ten – **Zen –** Golden Rock	

STEP 4

Now that you have memorized the above pairs, recall the objects in order.

1. _____
2. _____
3. _____
4. _____
5. _____
6. _____
7. _____
8. _____
9. _____
10. _____

STEP 5

Let's repeat the previous exercise, but change up the order. Which object is:

8. _____
10. _____
7. _____
5. _____
2. _____
3. _____
1. _____
9. _____
4. _____
6. _____

Step 6.

Wait until tomorrow and see how many of the objects you can recall in order. Repeat this a week from now. You will be amazed at what your mind can do.

Step 7.

If you want to memorize lists that have more than 10 items, you can stack the rhymes. For example:

Objects to remember in order:

   11. Football
   12. Baseball cap
   13. Kayak
   14. Rose

First, let's take the 11th item, a football. Take the rhymes for 10 (Zen) + 1 (Sun). Imagine the Sun meditating over a football field.

12th item, a baseball cap: Take Zen (10) + Blue (2) and associate it with someone sticking out of a mediation group because they didn't take off their blue baseball cap.

13th item: a kayak. Take Zen (10) + Tree (3) and associate it with someone kayaking in the sand of a Zen Garden under a tree.

14th item: a rose. Take Zen (10) + Door (4) and associate it with the door of a very Zen monastery opening and someone handing you a rose.

This works for any number combination. Let's take 98. The 98th item is carrots. Take the rhyme for 9 (wine) + 8 (date) and associate it with someone getting so sloshed on wine on a date that they throw up their carrots from their salad. Gross? Yes! Memorable? Also, yes.

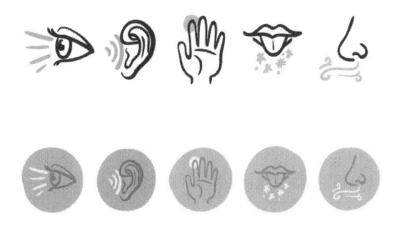

Figure 1 - To maximize memory always use the 5 senses

The more absurd the image including violent, bizarre, funny or sexual, the more likely you will remember. One theory over why memory stopped being taught in schools since ancient Greek times was that religious sects found this method of conjuring up inappropriate images unholy.

While inappropriate images may easier to remember, this is not a must if it's outside your comfort zone. You can just as easily conjure up vivid images that don't offend your sense of propriety.

Use all your senses. Imagine the scene in vivid colors, either really aromatic or stinky smells, weird textures & strange noises. E.g. If you are thinking of the ocean, feel the breeze on your face and the sand beneath your feet. Hear the sound of the waves crashing. Taste the salt in the air from the sea.

The Shape System

The Shape System is an alternative to the Peg/Rhyme System. It converts numbers into shapes.

My personal preference is the Peg/Rhyme System but I want you to be aware of this option as well as depending on your personal learning style, one method may work more effectively for you.

Figure 2 - The Shape System - Numbers shaped like animals

Ex. Let's take the same list as the Peg System to memorize with the Shape System:

Items we want to remember in this order:

1. Duck
2. Movie
3. Goat
4. Frog
5. Goggles
6. Helmet
7. Ladder
8. Robot
9. Owl
10. Golden Rock

In this case you would need to associate the item to be memorized with the shape associated with a given number.

So..

Now we need to come up with some memorable imagery. Why don't you take a crack at it and then compare with the answer on the next page?

According to our "Shape System" above:

- 1 = Meerkat
- 2 = Swan
- 3 = Turtle
- 4 = Ostrich
- 5 = Peacock
- 6 = Fox
- 7 = Toucan
- 8 = Snake
- 9 = Raccoon
- 0 = Penguin

Composite image to remember our list by tying in the Shape System images:

1. A duck attacking a Meerkat
2. A swan checking out an outdoor movie by the lake
3. A goat jumping on the shell of a turtle who is resting in the shape of a number 3 (see picture on previous page).
4. A frog being eaten by a flamingo
5. A peacock wearing goggles
6. A fox wearing a protective helmet
7. A toucan walking up a ladder because his wings are injured
8. A snake coiling around a robot
9. An owl who is trying to snatch a raccoon
10. A penguin and a meerkat building a nest out of golden rocks

This is also a great system for visual learners to memorize short lists.

In order to memorize much longer and complex numbers, we will move onto the Major System in the next chapter.

Chapter 6:
The Major System

The Major System, thought to have been named after, Major Beniowski[x] (although some dispute this origin), is a phonetic system that links sounds to numerical value.

Because it is a phonetic system, the most important factor is the sound of the consonant, not the spelling. This is very important, we are using a system based on sound, not the actual spelling.

You do not need to be a trained linguist to learn this system. All it takes is practice.

The Major System was first published by Aime Paris[xi] in its modern form but is believed to have been revised over hundreds or possibly even thousands of years.

It is also known as Herigone's Mnemonic System. The human brain tends to remember words and associated images much better than numbers, in fact, the more vivid, violent and outrageous the image, the better the brain remembers it.

Contestants at Memory Competitions tend to have developed their own methods based on ancient memory systems. Most of people taking part in memory competitions are reluctant to reveal their memory techniques for obvious reasons. In the Superhuman Memory System, I bring you my own proverbial "secret sauce".

Once you master the below numerical and sound pairs, you are well on your way to laying a very important foundation of the Superhuman Memory Program.

Here is a quick summary of the sound-based Major System:

It might seem overwhelming to some but not to worry, we will go over it in much detail in the next few chapters. There are also a number of videos in the bonus area to explain this in the easiest way possible.

The Major System Table

Number	Sound	Ways to Recall	Examples
0	S, soft C, Z	Zero begins with the /z/ sound	Ice, Sauce, zero
1	T, D, TH	T and D have one vertical stroke, as the number 1.	Tie, Dye, This
2	N	The letter N has two vertical strokes.	No, Knee
3	M	The lower case letter m has three vertical strokes. The lower case m also looks like a 3 on its side.	Moo, Me, Home
4	R	Four ends with the letter "R".	Row
5	L	The Roman numeral for L is 50.	Lei, Loo, Law
6	Ch, Sh, Sch, Tsch, Cz, J, S (tissue)	The lower case letter g looks like an upside down 6. The letter J can also hold a 6 in its hook.	Shoe, Chew, Cheese, Cello, Seizure, Putsch, Giant, Jury, Schnitzel, Czech
7	K, hard C, Q, G	The letter K looks like 2 sevens linked together.	Key, Goat, Game, Cake
8	F, Ph, V	A lower case "f" resembles the number 8.	UFO, Few, View, Phone, Faux
9	P, B	A lower case p resembles the number 9 if flipped.	Bee, Pool
No value	H, Y, W, Vowels (A, E, I, O, U)	When the consonant is not pronounced, do not assign it a numerical value.	Ex. In "Law" the "w" is silent. The vowel "a" is skipped. In "Home" – the H and vowels are silent.

Chunking

The Major System deals with 1 and 2 digit number pegs. When you are trying to memorize strings of numbers, it helps to break them down into pieces. This is the same reason why phone numbers are broken into chunks.

Step 1. Take a look at the following number: 1914193917761917

Does it seem overwhelming? If you don't even want to bother trying to memorize it, you are not alone. It is daunting. Trying to memorize something like this without chunking through simple rote memory may give you a headache, which is why I want you to try it the easy way.

Step 2. What about now? Does it seem more manageable? 1914-1939-1776-1917

Step 3. Let's give the numbers more meaning:

1914 – the year World War I started
1939 – the year World War II started
1776 – US Independence
1917 – The Russian Revolution

We will break long strings of numbers down into chunks throughout this course. In the above example, it was easy to give meaning to chunks of numbers.

In the following lesson, we will learn the Major System, where we will convert numbers into sounds and those sounds into words and images.

This is the best way to give meaning to numbers that otherwise wouldn't particularly be memorable.

Ways to Remember the Major System

Zero converts to the s or z sounds and is easy to remember because begins with the /z/ sound.

Example: The word "I**c**e" converts to a zero value based on the "s" sound. Note that vowels are ignored.

Figure 3 - Ice = Major System Ex. for 0

Other Major System values for Zero (0) include but are not limited to: use, ways, essay, Oz, see, sea, ouzo, soy, Soho

The number One (1) stands for the t or d sounds.

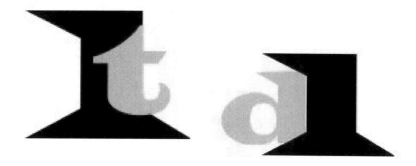

You can remember them easily as the letters "T" and "D" both have one vertical stroke in them, as does the number 1.

Example. The word "**T**i**e**" converts to a major system value of 1. We ignore the vowels. Other examples of words that convert to "1" include **d**ye, **t**oe, **d**oe, ha**t**. **Vowels and the consonants h, y, w and x are ignored.**

Figure 4 - Tie = Major System Value of 1

Other Major System values for One (1) include but are not limited to: ai**d**, **d**ay, i**d**ea, **t**he, **t**wo, **d**ie, I**d**aho, **D**oha, i**t**, ha**t**e, o**dd**, awai**t**, how**d**y.

> **Note**: Occasionally you may find that various teaching methods or online Major System Generators have slight differences in interpreting the Major System.

Two converts to the "N" sound.

The letter N has two vertical strokes.

An example of a Major System number to word conversion is Honey.
Note, we ignore the vowels as well as h, w, x and y.

Figure 5 - Honey = Major System 2 Conversion

Other Major System values for Two (2) include but are not limited to: **N**oah, A**nn**a, Ha**nn**ah, a**nn**oy, **n**o, Ia**n**, **n**ow, io**n**, Iowa**n**, Ha**n**oi, he**nn**a

Three converts to the m sound. This is also very easy to remember as a lower case letter "m" has three vertical strokes.

The lower case letter m has three vertical strokes. The lower case m also looks like a 3 on its side.

An Example of a Major System number to word conversion is "**Moo**". Again, as in previous examples, we ignore the vowels.

Figure 6 - 3 - Moo Major System Example

Other Major System values for Three (3) include but are not limited to: **M**aui, **m**eow, ai**m**, O**m**aha, E**mm**a, ha**m**, **m**ayo, **m**e, **M**ao

Four converts to the "R" sound. This is also very easy to remember as "four" ends in the letter "r".

Four ends with the letter "R".

Major system example: **R**ow. As per Major System rules, we ignore the vowel and the "w".

Figure 7 - Row converts to 4 per the Major System

Other Major System values for Four (4) include but are not limited to: Eu**r**o, **R**io, hu**rr**y, He**r**a, wa**r**, **r**aw, ai**r**way, he**r**e and hou**r**.

X XX XXX XL L
10 20 30 40 50

The Roman numeral for L is 50. (Yes, "L" in Roman numerals is larger than "XL", contrary to our clothing sizing.). The X's above are the Roman Numeral equivalents. In this version of the Major System, I recommend that you don't assign the letter "x" a sound value.

Example. Lei is a word that converts to 5. Again, vowels are ignored.

Figure 8 - Lei is a word that converts to 5 under Major System rules

Other Major System values for Five (5) include but are not limited to: Owl, aloha, Leah, hell, hall, law, hole and Lao.

6 giant
6 J Joker

An upside down lower-case letter "g" looks like a 6. Remember, when using the Major System, we actually go by the sound – so while a "g" as pronounced in the word "giant" would translate to a 6, a hard "g" as in the word goat, would translate to a 7. Also, a 6 can easily fit into the hook of a letter J.

Example. 6 converts to the word **Sh**oe. The way I personally remember that 6 stands for the **TSCH, SCH, SH** sounds is that I think of a woman's **shoe with 6-inch heels**.

Figure 9 - Shoe converts to the value 6 under the Major System

Other Major System values for Six (6) include but are not limited to: **J**oey, **j**oy, a**sh**, wa**sh**, **ch**i, ha**sh**, **sh**y, **j**aw, **g**em

The letter "K" kind of resembles two twisted 7's. Remember, in the Major System we go by sound. So the letter "C" in words like Cake is a hard c, which sounds like the letter "k". An example of a soft "c" sound would be race – here the "c" sound would convert to a zero.

Therefore "Cake" translates to 77. A hard "G" also translates to a 7. An example of a hard "g" would be the "g" in goat.

Example. The word **K**ey converts to the number 7.

Figure 10 - The word key converts to 7 as per Major System rules

Other Major System values for Seven (7) include but are not limited to: wea**k**, o**k**ay, ha**k**u, ho**ck**ey, hi**ck**ey, a**q**ua, I**Q**, e**c**o

The number eight resembles a lower case cursive letter "f".

An example of a number to word conversion for the number 8, is UFO – we ignore the vowels as per Major System rules.

Figure 11 - UFO converts to the number 8

Other Major System values for Eight (8) include but are not limited to: i**v**y, **v**iew, hu**ff**, hi-**f**i, **f**ew, **f**aux, E**v**a, E**v**e.

The number 9 resembles the letters "p" and lower case "b" once rotated in a similar direction.

Example. The word "bee" converts to the numerical value 9. We ignore the vowels as per Major System rules.

Figure 12 - Bee converts to 9 under Major System rules

Other Major System values for Nine (0) include but are not limited to: hu**b**, **p**ie, o**b**ey, **b**uy, hu**b**, A**bb**y, a**pp**, a**p**e and **B**owie.

Recap of the Major System

Number	Sound	Ways to Recall	Examples
0	S, soft C, Z	Zero begins with the /z/ sound	Ice, Sauce, zero
1	T, D, TH	T and D have one vertical stroke, as the number 1.	Tie, Dye, This
2	N	The letter N has two vertical strokes.	No, Knee
3	M	The lower case letter m has three vertical strokes. The lower case m also looks like a 3 on its side.	Moo, Me, Home
4	R	Four ends with the letter "R".	Row
5	L	The Roman numeral for L is 50.	Lei, Loo, Law
6	Ch, Sh, Sch, Tsch, Cz, J, S (tissue)	The lower case letter g looks like an upside down 6. The letter J can also hold a 6 in its hook.	Shoe, Chew, Cheese, Cello, Seizure, Putsch, Giant, Jury, Schnitzel, Czech
7	K, hard C, Q, G	The letter K looks like 2 sevens linked together.	Key, Goat, Game, Cake
8	F, Ph, V	A lower case "f" resembles the number 8.	UFO, Few, View, Phone, Faux

9	P, B	A lower case p resembles the number 9 if flipped.	Bee, Pool
No value	H, Y, W, Vowels (A, E, I, O, U)	When the consonant is not pronounced, do not assign it a numerical value.	Ex. In "Law" the "w" is silent. The vowel "a" is skipped. In "Home" – the H and vowels are silent.

Ex. 1.

Let's do a basic recap of the Major System based on the above reference table. Every number has a variety of words it could represent, but every word can only be translated into one number. For example:

Robot = 491

R= 4
B=9
T-1

The Major System is based on sounds as described in the above table. The vowels are not converted into numerical equivalents.

Double consonants are also converted into a single number. While the word "robot" will always covert to the numerical value of 491.

Ex. 2.

491 = Rabbit
491 = Robot
491 = Orbit
491= Ripped
491 = Warped
491 = Repaid
491= Rowboat

RABBIT = 491

ORBIT = 491

ROBOT = 491

This also comes in handy when remembering phone numbers.

Ex. 3

You can make up complex words from numbers if you wish, however the process is much easier vice versa.

For example, it is easy to convert "komodo dragon" into a number, however, it is much easier and faster to convert the composite number broken down into double and a single word image.

Remember, vowels and the consonants h, x, y and w are silent. Double letters (the same letter twice next to each other) also count as a single sound. E.g. **Rabbit** = 491, not 4991. The "bb" converts to a single value for the number 9.

731-1472 = KOMODO DRAGON

Figure 13 - Komodo dragon

Remember Dates

2012 = EINSTEIN
1979 = TOPGAP
1950 = TABLES
2001 = NICEST
1920 = ETHIOPIANS

If you have tried to convert 3 and 4 digit numbers such as years on your own, you can attest that this is no easy task. For this reason, we will focus on two digit number conversions using the major system.

Note, numbers can be converted into a variety of words using the Major System, but not vice versa.

In the interest of instant recall, it is best to have a variety of images ready. The most effective way to memorize these images is to cut out the below table and practice the conversion of numbers into images.

When you reach the advanced level, you will have memorized a noun, a verb and an adjective for each single and double-digit number.

To start out with, you will memorize a number for each single and double-digit number based on the Major System.

This is completely manageable; the total comes to 108 number, word/image associations.

It may seem like an excessive amount of up-front work, as long as you practice these images, you will have a lifelong numerical memory library to fall back on.

The key is to incorporate them into your life on a daily basis.

Note that the Major System is a <u>phonetic</u> system. The above table assumes US/Canadian English pronunciation. E.g CaR would be 74 as both the hard C and the letter R are pronounced.

You may encounter slight differences in how people apply the Major System. I would recommend that you go by your own pronunciation.

Also, we should mention the letter "X". In some variations of the Major System the letter "X" is unassigned, while others go with the pronunciations and assign value as if it were "KS" thus 70.

For example, the word FOX could be either 8 or 870. For simplicity's sake, I recommend not assigning values to X so x = unassigned/has no value.

If you enter the number 8 into the following online mnemonic generator http://major-system.info/, you will get results such as fox, fix and fax[xii]. Here the x has no assigned value.

The letters Y and W in the English language are also known as semi-vowels. Y (as in "yes) and W (as in West) are close to *ee* and *oo* vowel sounds[xiii].

What is important when mastering the Major System is consistency.

Chapter 7:
Creating Effective Passwords

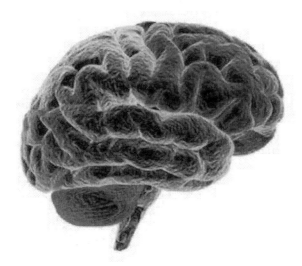

A fantastic application of the Major System is developing complex passwords. Most people will not remember long strings of numbers with no real meaning to them.

However, take a meaningful quote and convert it to numbers, you have a formidable passwords. It's best to chose something that is not familiar even to those close to us. E.g. if you are crazy for Harry Potter and everyone knows it, don't incorporate it as part of your password.

Ex. 1. "The best revenge is massive success."
– Frank Sinatra

Let's take a look at the breakdown. As you progress in the course, you will be able to convert text into numbers effortlessly. For beginners, I recommend printing off the Major System chart for reference.

"The best revenge is massive success"
1   9 01 4 8 26   0 3   0 8   0 7   0

Note: The vowels have been skipped and consecutive double letters convert into a single number. For example, the double "c" and the double "s" convert to a single number in the above example.

Note: The letter "g" in the word "revenge" is not a hard G. We need to go by sound, where it falls into the category assigned to the number 6.

Voila! You have your formidable password, just combine it with an easy to remember letter and symbol combination.

Ex 2. "Whatever you are, be a good one."
– Abraham Lincoln

"Whatever you are, be a good one."
1 8 4   4   9   7 1 2

The above password combinations are even more powerful if you mix it with words and symbols, in fact, for most websites you will need to mix them up with letters and symbols, but the most difficult to guess part will be the number combination.

I tend to pick a quote that has some special meaning to me and some kind of a relevance as to what I need the password for – for example, pick a quote associated for wealth or success for finance related passwords. We will spend more time discussing alphanumeric character combinations in the latter part of the book.

"I have no special talents. I am only passionately curious."
— *Albert Einstein*

Chapter 8:
Practice with Mind Maps

One of the best ways to wrap your head around the Major System is mind-maps. I love technology but every once in a while pen and paper just help with the creative process. Tony Buzan is credited with the invention of mind maps[xiv].

Whether you are learning mnemonics or you are brainstorming your next big project at work or trying to decide between options on how to remodel your house, mind-mapping will help you, especially if you are the scribbling type, like I am.

You can use a smartphone app as there are many. You can use free or premium online software or a good old fashioned paper and the back of a napkin from your kitchen.

Exercise: Take a piece of paper, write down a 1-2 digit number in the center circle and come up with as many possibilities of Major System conversions that you can think of.

For example:

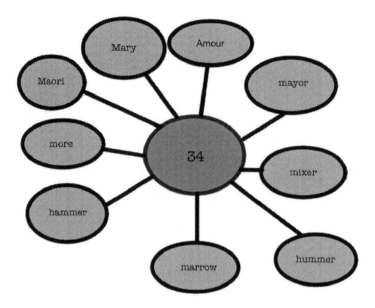

Figure 14 - Mind Map of Major System Conversion of 34

If pen and paper is not your thing, there are a number of Mind Map Apps available for your smartphone. The below Mind Maps were created with a graphics tablet, which is also a great tool if you are an illustrator or just dabbling in digital art but there is nothing more convenient and easy than pen and paper.

The below image is a Mind Map for zero (0). As you recall from the Major System table above, zero is associated with the S, soft c, z & x sounds.

Remember, vowels and the consonants h, x, w and y have no assigned value.

Figure 15 - Mind Map for Major System conversion for Zero Mind Map Double Zero (00)

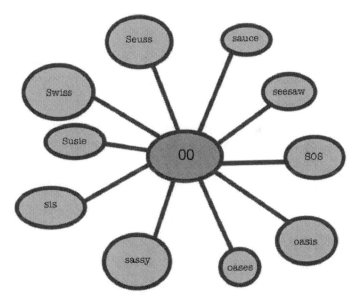

Figure 16 - Mind Map for Major System conversion of Double Zero

Let's also do a mind map with our random one-digit number, 6.

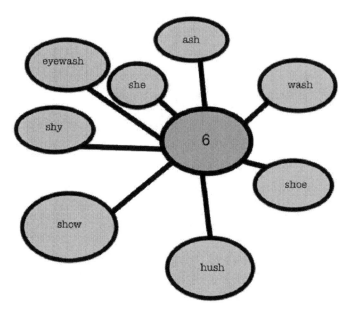

Figure 17 - Mind Map for Major System conversions of 6

Now onto a random 3-digit number: 275

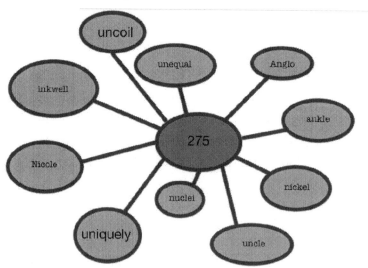

Figure 18 - Mind Map of Major System conversion of the number 275

If you tried to convert the 3-digit number into words on your own, you can see how as the numbers get larger, it is more and more difficult to come up with a single word conversion for a single number.

If you proceed to 4-digit numbers, you will see how it becomes even more challenging to accomplish the task. Therefore, it is better to stick to one and two digit numbers and make composites of them, the longer the number, the more likely you will need to come up with a story to remember it.

For this reason, in this method, we will focus on converting single and double- digit numbers using a pre-drawn image library.

Chapter 9:
Major System Imagery

When it comes to quick memorization of numbers, it is best to have a ready library that immediately comes to mind. While, eventually you will have your own library of images, especially meaningful to you, I find it much easier to have a ready-made image library to start out with.

ACTION RECOMMENDED: I recommend that you print the Major System Study Cards from the Bonus Download page of the Members Area on Memoryprofessor.com, cut them up into notecards and study them over the next 30 days.

Just 5-10 minutes/day will allow for impressive progress. 5 minutes/day will also leave you with very rewarding results.

You will see how as you go through your day, you will convert account numbers, license plates and other numbers into images. Repetition is key to memorization. Whatever you want to store in long-term memory, will need to be practiced over and over again at intervals.

"Genius is 1% talent and 99% percent hard work..."
— *Albert Einstein*

One question I often get asked is whether photographic memory really exists? And if it does exist, can we acquire it?

This question has fascinated experts for a long time.

It depends on how you define photographic memory. If it is recalling an event or page in a book from memory that you only glanced at once, then mentally zooming in to look for any tiny detail – then it doesn't really exist.

If you think of it as remembering an extraordinary amount of information that was consciously memorized, then it absolutely does.

There are individuals who seem to possess uncanny abilities to remember a seemingly impossible amount of information.

In most of these cases, they do not possess abilities that you and I do not. They are just simply using memory techniques to retain information that otherwise is arbitrary.

Human beings are exceptional when it comes to remembering faces, images and also do incredibly well when it comes to spatial orientation.

Memory Championships are held world-wide where competitors test their skill against one another. In most cases, they were born with average abilities when it comes to memory.

Remember when you were learning to read, speak another language, type or drive? At first it took a lot of effort and concentration but soon you were able to do it without effort?

It takes a bit more time and effort to learn, but is well worth it! In no time, when you see a number, you will automatically see the image associated with it in this lesson.

It's not quite the photographic memory some hope to acquire but is as close as we can get and almost every bit as impressive, especially as so few people are able/willing to truly master it.

Now, let's get to work on the Major System. This is the most effective and most important skill for you to learn if you want to instantly memorize anything having to do with numbers or out of sequence lists.

In the following pages, you will see a single or double digit number, a word with a sound to number value conversion and an image.

Major System Illustrations

Number – Major System Sound Conversion – Image

00	SauCe Major System Sound S=0 C=0	
01	SoDa Major System Sound S=0 D=1	
02	SuN Major Syste Sound S=0 N=2	

03	SuMo **Major System Sound** S=0 m=3	
04	SieRRa[1] **Major System Sound** S=0 r=4	
05	SoiL **Major System Sound** S=0 l=5	

06	SuSHi **Major System Sound** S=0 sh=6	
07	SoCK **Major System Sound** S=0 ck=7	
08	SoFa **Major System Sound** S=0 f=8	

09	SoaP **Major System Sound** S=0 p=9	

Exercise 00 -09

Write down the corresponding image to the following:

02 _____

04 _____

03 _____

06 _____

00 _____

09 _____

07 _____

06 _____

01 _____

Convert this number into imagery:

01090506

***Answer**: Ready made images corresponding to the two-digit numbers: Soda (01) , Soap (09), Soil (05), Sushi (06).

Example of a single image to memorize all images: You're at a BBQ and you are drinking <u>soda</u>, then slip on <u>soap</u>, falling onto the <u>soil</u> and knocking over a tray of <u>sushi</u>.

Single Digit Major System conversions from 0 to 9.

0 (Zero)	iCe Major System Sound C = 0	
1	Tie **Major System Sound t=1**	
2	HoNey **Major System Sound N=2**	

3	Moo **Major System Sound M=3**	
4	Row² **Major System Sound R=4**	
5	Lei **Major System Sound l=5**	

6	SHoe **Major System Sound Sh=6**	
7	Key **Major System Sound K=7**	
8	UFO[3] **Major System Sound F=8**	

9	Bee **Major System Sound** **B=9**	
10	oaTS **Major System Sound** **T=1** **S=0**	

Exercise 00-9

Write down the name of the corresponding image to the following:

02 _____

8 _____

01 _____

5 _____

7 _____

03 _____

3 _____

6 _____

00 _____

0 _____

2 _____

4 _____

07 _____

06 _____

07 _____

9 _____

11	TuTu[4] **Major System Sound** T=1 T=1	
12	TuNa **Major System Sound** T=1 N=2	
13	TiMe **Major System Sound** t=1 m=3	

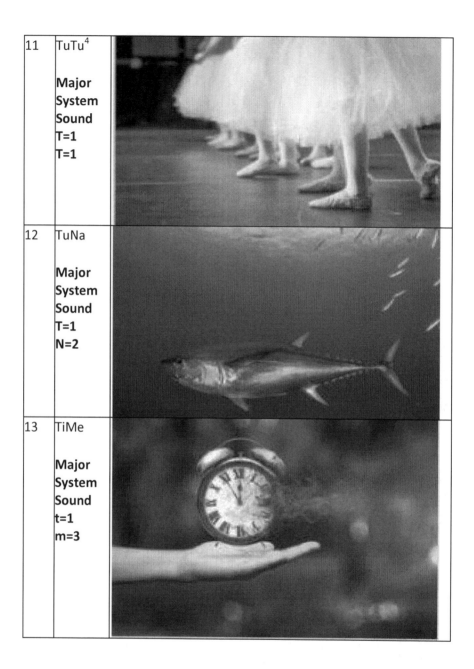

14	DooR **Major System Sound** d=1 r=4	
15	DoLL[5] **Major System Sound** d=1 l=5	
16	DiSH **Major System Sound** d=1 sh=6	

17	ToGa **Major System Sound** **T=1** **G=7**	
18	ToFu **Major System Sound** **T=1** **F=8**	
19	TuB **Major System Sound** **T=1** **b=9**	

Exercise 10 -19

Write down the name of the corresponding image to the following:

11 _____

19 _____

17 _____

13 _____

10 _____

12 _____

14 _____

15 _____

16 _____

18 _____

20	NaSa **Major System Sound N=2 s=0**	
21	NoTe **Major System Sound N=2 T=1**	
22	NuN **Major System Sound N=2 N=2**	

23	GNoMe[6] **Major System Sound** (G)n=2 M=3	
24	NoRway[7] **Major System Sound** N=2 R=4	
25	NaiL **Major System Sound** N=2 L=5	

26	NaCHo **Major System Sound N=2 Ch=6**	
27	NeCK **Major System Sound N=2 K=7**	
28	NaVy **Major System Sound N=2 V=8**	

| 29 | NaP

Major System Sound N=2 P=9 |  |

Exercise 20 -29

Write down the name of the corresponding image to the following:

21 _____

29 _____

27 _____

23 _____

20 _____

22 _____

24 _____

25 _____

26 _____

28 _____

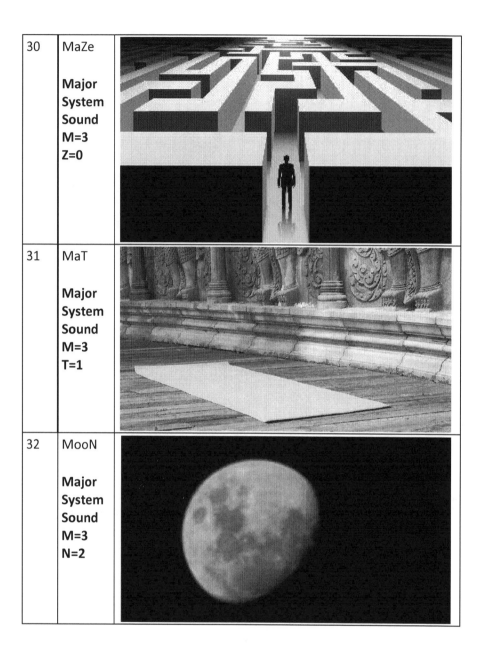

30	MaZe **Major** **System** **Sound** **M=3** **Z=0**	
31	MaT **Major** **System** **Sound** **M=3** **T=1**	
32	MooN **Major** **System** **Sound** **M=3** **N=2**	

33	MoM **Major System Sound M=3 M=3**	
34	MayoR **Major System Sound M=3 R=4**	
35	MaiL **Major System Sound M=3 L=5**	

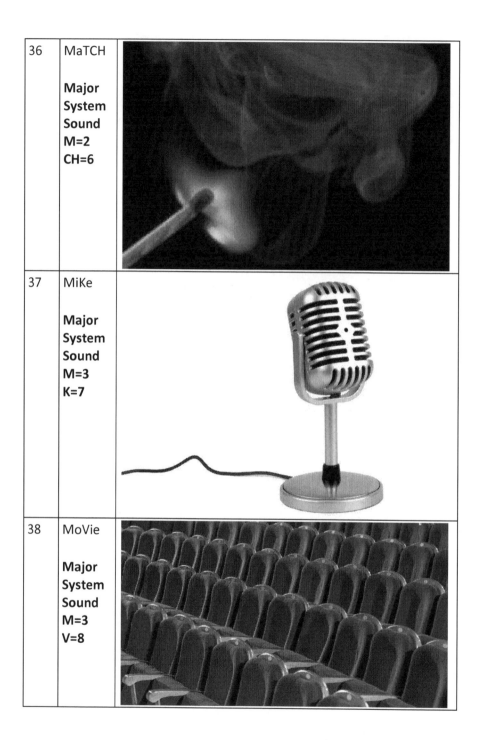

36	MaTCH **Major System Sound** **M=2** **CH=6**
37	MiKe **Major System Sound** **M=3** **K=7**
38	MoVie **Major System Sound** **M=3** **V=8**

| 39 | MaP

Major System Sound M=3 p=9 | 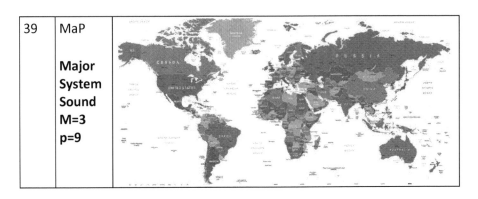 |

Exercise 30 -39

Write down the name of the corresponding image to the following:

31 _____

39 _____

37 _____

33 _____

30 _____

32 _____

34 _____

35 _____

36 _____

38 _____

40	RiCe **Major System Sound** r=4 c=0	
41	RaT **Major System Sound** r=4 t=1	
42	RuN **Major System Sound** r=4 n=2	

43	RuM **Major System Sound** r=4 m=3	
44	auRoRa **Major System Sound** r=4 r=4	

45	RaiL **Major System Sound** r=4 5=l	
46	RoaCH **Major System Sound** r=4 ch=6	
47	RaKe **Major System Sound** r=4 k=7	

48	ReeF **Major System Sound** r=4 k=7	
49	RoBe **Major System Sound** r=4 b=9	

Exercise 40 -49

Write down the name of the corresponding image to the following:

41 _____

49 _____

47 _____

43 _____

40 _____

42 _____

44 _____

45 _____

46 _____

48 _____

50	LiCe **Major System Sound** l=5 c=0	
51	LiD **Major System Sound** l=5 d=1	
52	LioN **Major System Sound** l=5 n=2	

53	LooM **Major System Sound R** l=5 m=3	
54	LiaR **Major System Sound** l=5 r=4	
55	LiLLy **Major System Sound** l=5 l=5	

56	LeeCH **Major System Sound** **L=5** **Ch=6**	
57	LuCK **Major System Sound** **L=5** **(C)k= 7**	
58	LiFe **Major System Sound** **L=5** **F=8**	

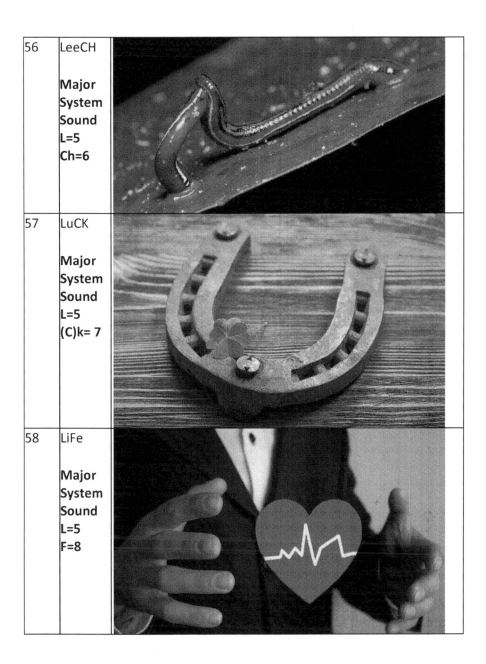

59	LiP Major System Sound L=5 P=9	

Exercise 50 -59

Write down the name of the corresponding image to the following:

51 _____

59 _____

57 _____

53 _____

50 _____

52 _____

54 _____

55 _____

56 _____

58 _____

53. _____

60	CHeeSe **Major System Sound Ch=6 S=0**	
61	CHaTeaux **Major System Sound Ch=6 T=1**	
62	CHiN **Major System Sound Ch=6 N=2**	

107

63	CHiMe **Major System Sound Ch=6 M=3**	
64	CHaiR **Major System Sound Ch=6 R=4**	
65	CHiLL **Major System Sound Ch=6 L=5**	

66	CHowCHow **Major System Sound Ch=6 Ch=6**	
67	CHeCK **Major System Sound ch=6 k=7**	
68	CHeF **Major System Sound ch=6 f=8**	

69	CHiP Major System Sound Sh=6 P=9	

Exercise 60 -69

Write down the name of the corresponding image to the following:

61 _____

69 _____

67 _____

63 _____

60 _____

62 _____

64 _____

65 _____

66 _____

68 _____

70	QuiZ **Major System Sound** **Q=7** **Z=0**	
71	KiD **Major System Sound** **K=7** **D=1**	
72	CaN **Major System Sound** **C=7 N=2**	

73	CoMMa **Major System Sound C=7 M=3**	
74	CaR **Major System Sound K=7 R=4**	
75	KaLe **Major System Sound K=7 L=5**	

76	CaSH **Major System Sound** **C=7** **Sh=6**	
77	CaKe **Major System Sound** **K=7** **K=7**	
78	CoFFee **Major System Sound** **C=7** **F=8**	

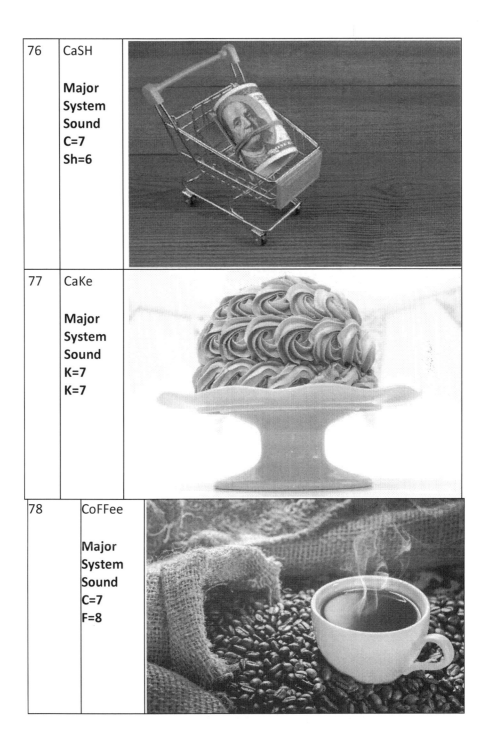

| 79 | CaP

Major System Sound
C=7
P=9 |  |

Exercise 70 -79

Write down the name of the corresponding image to the following:

71 _____

79 _____

77 _____

73 _____

70 _____

72 _____

74 _____

75 _____

76 _____

78 _____

70 _____

80	VaSe **Major System Sound** **V=8** **S=0**	
81	FiT **Major System Sound** **F=8** **T=1**	
82	PHoNe **Major System Sound** **Ph=8** **N=2**	

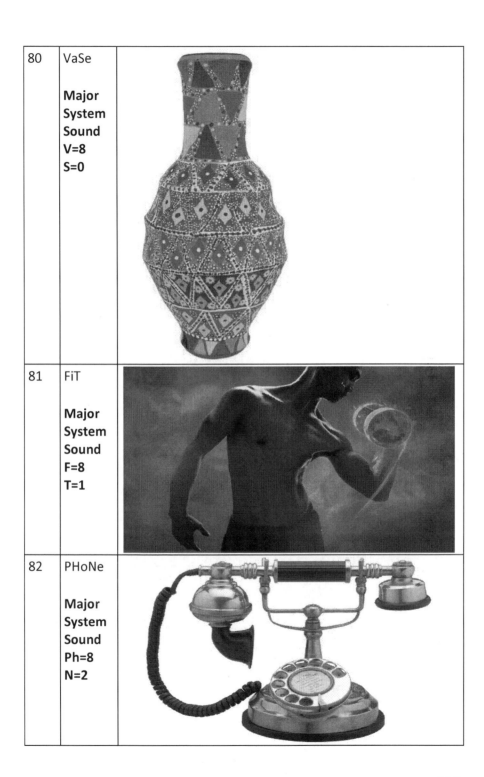

83	FoaM **Major System Sound** F=8 M=3	
84	FiRe **Major System Sound** F=8 R=4	
85	FaLL **Major System Sound** F=8 L=5	

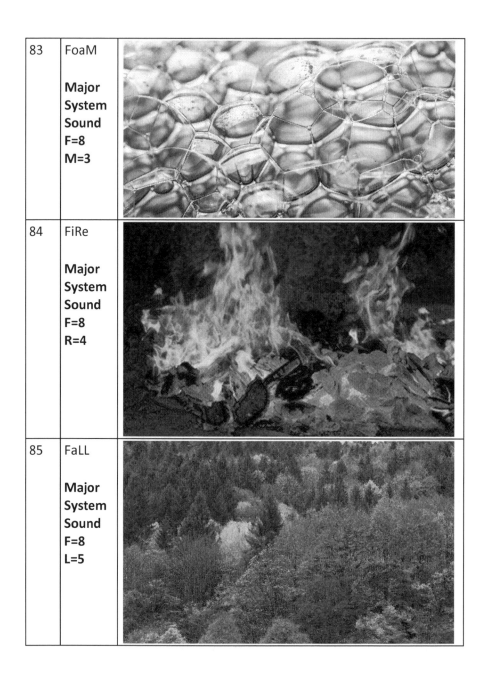

86	FiSH Major System Sound F=8 Sh=6	
87	FiG Major System Sound F=8 G=7	
88	ViVa Major System Sound V=8 V=8	

| 89 | ViBe

Major System Sound Major System Sound V=8 B=9 | 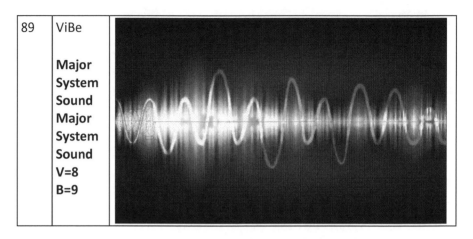 |

Exercise 80 -89

Write down the name of the corresponding image to the following:

81 _____

89 _____

87 _____

83 _____

80 _____

82 _____

84 _____

85 _____

86 _____

88 _____

90	BoSS **Major System Sound B=9 S=0**	
91	BeD **Major System Sound B=9 D=1**	
92	BuN **Major System Sound B=9 D=1**	

93	PuMa **Major System Sound** **P=9** **M=3**	
94	PeaR **Major System Sound** **P=9** **R=4**	
95	PooL **Major System Sound** **P=9** **L=5**	

96	PeaCH **Major System Sound** **p=9** **ch=6**	
97	BaCK **Major System Sound** **B=9** **k=7**	

98	BeeF **Major System Sound** **B=9** **f=8**	
99	BiB **Major System Sound** **B=9** **B=9**	

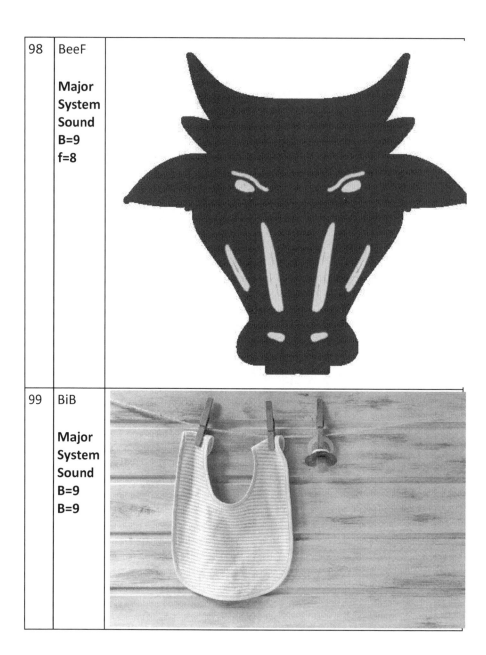

Exercise 90 -99

Write down the name of the corresponding image to the following:

91 _____

99 _____

97 _____

93 _____

90 _____

92 _____

94 _____

95 _____

96 _____

98 _____

Soon enough, when you see 22 you will immediately think of a Nun, with 33, Mom, 99 Bib etc. You will think in pictures without even trying. All it takes is regular practice.

"Every man's memory is his private literature."
— *Aldous Huxley*

Chapter 10:
Memory Palace or Loci Method to Remember digits of Pi

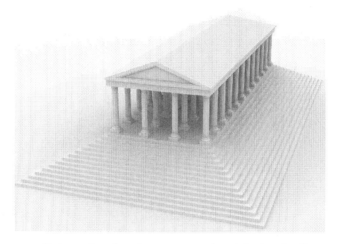

The Memory Palace is also known as the Method of Loci. It is a mental construct of a familiar physical location. Think back to your childhood home, a friend's house, a vacation home or your high school. Chances are, you will be able to do a mental walkthrough of spaces you used to frequent. Humans, in fact, have been known to be so called geospatial geniuses.

The history behind the term "Memory Palace" comes from Ancient Greece. Its factual authenticity has been doubted however, it makes for a good story. In Ancient Greece, Simonides of Ceos[xv] (c. 546 - 486 BCE) was giving a speech at a banquet.

He was called outside for some reason, and at that point, the building collapsed and everyone inside died.

Simonides is said to have been able to provide comfort to the families, by mentally reconstructing the banquet and identified the bodies of the deceased based on where he remembered everyone's location.

IMPORTANT: Memory is NOT photographic. It is creative. The more vivid, crazy, loud and outrageous you can make your mental image, the more you will be able to remember.

It may seem silly at first but you don't need to tell anyone what techniques you are using. The outside world will not see the creative process unless you choose to share.

Remember, in order to be effective, your walkthrough of your chosen Memory Palace should engage all senses:

- Sight,
- Sound,
- Touch,
- Taste and
- Smell.

The more vivid you make the images, the more you will remember.

The reason why you remember vivid images that stand out from the rest is called the Isolation Effect, also known as the Von Restorff Effect, coined by the German psychiatrist, Hedwig Von Restorff[xvi].

She discovered that when multiple homogenous items/stimuli are present, the one that stands out, is more likely to be remembered.

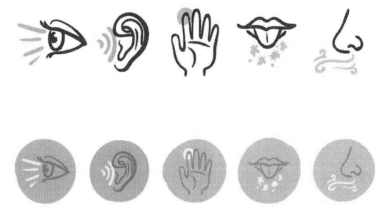

Figure 19 - Engage the 5 senses in your Memory Palace

Build Your Own Memory Palaces

Now let's build some of your own Memory Palaces. It does not have to be an actual palace. Any building where you are familiar with the interior and can do a detailed mental walk-through will do. Pick a location, best if it is a house or apartment familiar to you.

You will construct a number of Memory Palaces, make sure to pick them based on size and complexity as appropriate to what list or number you are attempting to memorize.

Suggestions for Memory Palaces:

- Your childhood home
- Your current home
- Your college dorm
- Your office
- Your high school or college campus
- The neighborhood grocery store
- A shopping mall you frequent
- The gym
- Your friend's house
- A cruise ship that you went on vacation on

Basically any location where you feel comfortable and know your surroundings will work as a Memory Palace. Chances are you can easily come up with at least 20 Memory Palaces.

Close your eyes and do a mental walk-through. Even if you haven't been to a place in over 30 years, if it was once familiar, you can easily imagine yourself walking from room to room.

This is one of the special gifts we have as humans. We just have a knack for remembering spaces.

Pick a variety of locations, from large to small so you will be able to accommodate your lists and numbers. For example, if you have a complex series of numbers to memorize, pick something bigger than a studio apartment.

Macro and Micro Locations

Loci is the plural form of the word locus, meaning a place where something is located/situated/occurs. Loci for the Memory Palace method fall into two categories: Macro Locations and Micro Locations.

A macro location can be a room such as a living room or bathroom in a house.

For example, here is a bird's eye view of an entire floor of a house. When you are familiar with a physical location, you can easily do a linear walk-through and imaging placing items from one room to another.

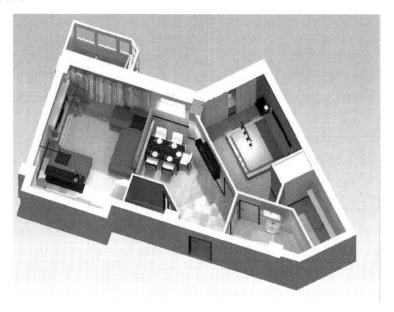

Figure 20: Memory Palace Example

A micro location is an item such as a piece of furniture inside a macro location.

As a beginner, I recommend starting out with only macro locations. If you are mentally doing a walk-through in your Memory Palace, it is important to have a clear linear and logical mental walkthrough.

It is best to sketch out your memory palaces with a list of macro and micro locations.

Exercise: Take out a piece of paper and write down two Memory Palaces you will use. You should have a list of macro and micro locations for both Memory Palaces.

A macro location can be a room such as a living room or bathroom. A micro location should be something that is fixed in a room such as a bed, shower or bathtub.

The Story Method

The key to remembering and passing on information for humans is creating stories. We love stories, we pay attention to them and we remember them.

A story connects important little details together that otherwise you would not remember.

We will mix the story method with the other mnemonic techniques in this book. The more complex the information, you are trying to memorize the more weaving in a story will help.

Make your memory come alive by thinking in vivid textural detail.

Cooking and Shopping Using Your Memory Palace

Here is a practical everyday use of the Memory Palace.

Let's say you are in the mood for tofu fajitas and need to go shopping.

Yes, you could just write the ingredients on a piece of paper, and if you are anything like me, you may forget to take the paper to the store and come home with at least 3 missing ingredients.

So, the ingredients are:
- Tofu (or chicken)
- Lime juice
- Olive oil
- Garlic
- Salt
- Ground cumin
- Chili powder
- Jalapeño pepper
- Cilantro
- Flour tortillas
- Avocado
- Sour Cream
- Bell peppers
- Canola oil
- Red onion

Imagine your home, there is tofu on legs/chicken outside your front door with 3 bell peppers (green, yellow and red). The bell peppers are ringing the bell. The chicken/tofu is reluctant to come in.

A pile of ground cumin is yelling "come in"! Mr. Avocado opens the door. As they enter, there is a strong odor of onions in the air. Mr. Tofu slips on some canola oil in the hallway, Mrs. Garlic puts salt on the oil on the floor so nobody else will slip.

In the kitchen, Mr. Jalapeño is making fun of the bell peppers that he is much stronger and scarier than them.

Chili powder who is homesick to his native Chile is telling the bell peppers not to worry because Jalapeño will be minced in no time.

The last thing Mr. Cilantro wants to hear is being chopped up. He offers everyone some refreshing lime-juice as it's very hot.

Sour cream is melting and can't stand the heat so retreats to the fridge.

In the living room, the tortillas are relaxing as they will come in very last in the cooking process. Everyone is wondering when Salsa, the life of the party will arrive.

It may seem like too much mental work to put in for a simple recipe or shopping list, however, it will become much quicker to put together stories and images like this.

Over time, you will be able to accomplish more and more complex memorization tasks using these methods.

Some people find it useful to include celebrities in their Memory Palaces. For example, if you are trying to remember ketchup, you can think of the Ketchup song by the Girl Band, Las Ketchup in your living room. If you want to pick up Pizza, think of Joey from Friends ringing the doorbell with pizza.

We will talk more about including celebrities of your choice to memorize numbers in the Advanced course when we put the technique together with the Major System.

Memorizing Digits of Pi Using a Memory Palace

Let's put our knowledge of Memory Palaces to use and memorize that might come in handy should you end up as a contestant on Jeopardy.

In the **Advanced Course**, I will teach you how to remember the first **100 decimals of Pi.** Yes, you heard that right! I will show you how to memorize 100 consecutive decimals of Pi.

Should you be interested in learning even more, by then, you will have the skills to learn much more.

For illustrative purposes, I have created a floor plan for you for memorizing the first 10 decimal digits of Pi. Here you see a linear walkthrough from

- Figure 1, the entrance, to
- Figure 2, the living room, to
- Figure 3, the kitchen, to
- Figure 4, the bedroom, to
- Figure 5, the bathroom.

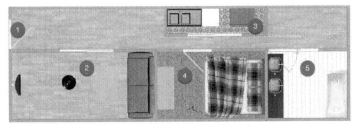

Figure 21 - Memory Palace Walkthrough[8]

Combining the Major System and Memory Palace Method

I find that when learning to use the Major System, it is much more meaningful to practice memorizing numbers that are meaningful either to you personally, like your credit card numbers or something that may one day come in handy on Jeopardy.

If you are the creative type, you can create your own 3D or 2D floor plans for your Memory Palace. The above floor plans were created using Roomsketcher.com.

π (Pi) is defined as a mathematical constant, the ratio of a circle's circumference to its diameter.

If you have not yet studied the Major System chapters (6-9), you should go back and at least do a thorough review.

It is also helpful to have your Major System study card cutouts (Bonus Download section).

Pi or π's first 10 decimals are:

3. 1415926535

Memory Palace Method, memorizing the first 10 digits of Pi

In this exercise, we will pick a memory palace with rooms as the macro locations.

Memory Palace Location: Home & Door
Number to remember: 3.14

Image: You arrive back at your childhood home. hoMe=**3**

Macro Locations in the house:

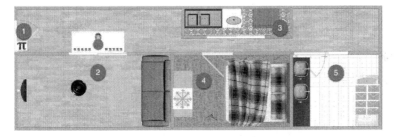

Walkthrough of Macro-locations inside the house aka "Memory Palace"

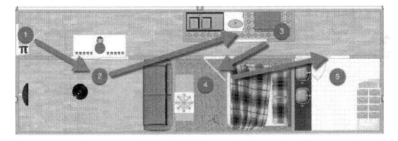

You get to the door (**DooR = 14**) which now has Pi on it instead of a house number. You open the door and walk into the hallway.

Memory Palace Location: Living Room
Number to remember 15
Major System number to word conversion: **DoLL** = 15
1=D, 5=L, O is silent as it's a vowel. Note: LL is not 55, just 5 as the Major System goes by sound, not all letters.

Image: a giant doll with surrounded, protected by a fence made up of π symbols). You are wondering why the heck there is a doll there and why it needs to be protected by a fence but you are interrupted by the delicious smell of freshly baked bread. You step across the Pi fence and follow the smell.

Memory Palace Location: Kitchen
Number to memorize: 92
Major System number to word conversion: **BuN b=9; n=2;** the vowel is silent

Image: Imagine walking into the kitchen and there is a freshly baked **bun**, with Pi on top of it, on top of the coffee table, imagine the smell of freshly baked bread.

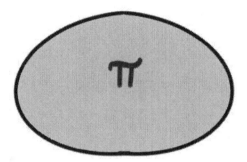

You are tired from your journey home and instead of eating in the kitchen, you head toward the bedroom.

Memory Palace Location: Bedroom
Number to remember: 65

Major System number to word conversion: **CHiLL** (CH = 6, 5=LL)
Image: The window is open and the room is freezing cold. The chill is so strong that you can see π shaped snowflakes in the room.

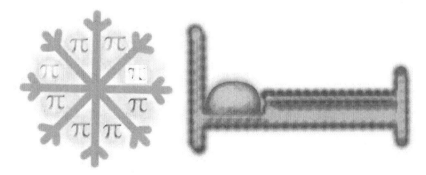

You want to go to sleep but you need to take a warm shower.

Memory palace location: Bathroom
Number to remember: 35
Major System number to word conversion: **MaiL (3 = M, 5=L, vowels silent)**
Image: You enter the bathroom and the bathtub is full of unopened letters.

Now mentally do a walk through of the entire house from the front door to the bathroom. You have just memorized the first 10 decimals of π.

Now you try it:

_. __ __ __ __ __

Answer:

3.1415926535

Congratulations! You've just memorized the first 10 decimals of Pi.

Pilish

If your primary objective is to memorize as many digits of Pi as humanly possible, there is another way.

Pilish is a style of writing where the number letters in each word correspond to a digit of Pi. This has nothing to do with the Major System – it just simply converts the number of letters in each word to a number. Now = 3 letters, I = 1 letter etc.

Michael Keith wrote a 10,000 word novella in Pilish, titled "*Not a Wake: A Dream Embodying π's Digits fully for the 10000 Decimals.*[xviii]"

Here are the first two lines of the book:

3   14 1 5   9   2 6   5   3 5
"Now I fall, a tired suburbian in liquid under the trees,

Drifting alongside forests simmering red in the twilight over Europe."
8   9   7   9   3 2 3 8   4   6

The Pi Master

In 2006, Akira Haraguchi from Japan recited 100,000 digits of Pi in 16 hours and 30 minutes[xix]. Can you believe that? One hundred thousand digits of Pi!

Does he have super human memory or special genes that allowed him to achieve this or did he develop a creative system to help him remember?

Correct, he developed a system to remember! He developed a system where he assigned Japanese Kana (syllabic Japanese scripts) to numbers and then memorized decimals of Pi as a collection of short stories.

This further proves that just because something seems near impossible, it doesn't mean that it can't be done. Maybe you just haven't found or applied the right method. As the old saying goes, "Where there is a will, there is a way".

Chapter 11:
Driving Directions and The Major System

Another great application of the Major System is memorizing driving directions. You can also combine this with the Memory Palace method in order to keep track of the order of directions but incorporating Major System images into a story works just as well.

While GPS technology is fantastic, I've learnt to have some backups just in case.. also, this way, I don't have to fiddle with my GPS/phone while driving.

Obviously, safety and concentration on the road is paramount. I would only recommend this method once you have truly mastered the Major System and the number-to-image conversions are automatic.

You want to concentrate on driving, not trying to remember what mnemonic image stands for what highway exit.

I devised it as a way for not having to fiddle with phones or maps, which takes your eyes off the road.

When you have a mental map with vivid imagery, you don't need to take your eyes off the road. Needless to say, do NOT close your eyes to recall images while driving.

I normally look up directions before heading out. I also have a list of Major System conversions for highways/interstates as well as relevant exits.

Here is the Major System Recap one more time:

Number	Sound	Ways to Recall	Examples
0	S, soft C, Z	Zero begins with the /z/ sound	Ice, Sauce, zero
1	T, D, TH	T and D have one vertical stroke, as the number 1.	Tie, Dye, This
2	N	The letter N has two vertical strokes.	No, Knee
3	M	The lower case letter m has three vertical strokes. The lower case m also looks like a 3 on its side.	Moo, Me, Home
4	R	Four ends with the letter "R".	Row
5	L	The Roman numeral for L is 50.	Lei, Loo, Law
6	Ch, Sh, Sch, Tsch, Cz, J, S (tissue)	The lower case letter g looks like an upside down 6. The letter J can also hold a 6 in its hook.	Shoe, Chew, Cheese, Cello, Seizure, Putsch, Giant, Jury, Schnitzel, Czech
7	K, hard C, Q, G	The letter K looks like 2 sevens linked together.	Key, Goat, Game, Cake
8	F, Ph, V	A lower case "f" resembles the number 8.	UFO, Few, View, Phone, Faux
9	P, B	A lower case p resembles the number 9 if flipped.	Bee, Pool
No value	H, Y, W, Vowels (A, E, I, O, U)	When the consonant is not pronounced, do not assign it a numerical value.	Ex. In "Law" the "w" is silent. The vowel "a" is skipped. In "Home" – the H and vowels are silent.

143

Now let's apply the Major System to driving directions. I recommend that you come up with a mental library of images for frequented routes, roads etc.

This should be done ahead of time. Like with every other application, this skill will also become automatic over time.

Example:

Interstate 395 is MaPLe.[9] (m=3; p=9; l=5; ignore the vowels)

I-495 = ReBeL (r=4; b=9; l=5; ignore the vowels)

Route 66 = ChowChow (as in the loveable furry dog breed) or the Song Route 66 (ch=6; ch=6; ignore vowels and w's)

101 = TeST (t=1; S=0; t=1)

For exits, I think of my car busting through a door:

Exit 505 = Car busting though a gate LouSiLy (LSL = 505).

I use the same techniques to remember street names as I do for people. However, do this well ahead of time, before you get into your car.

For example, let's take a fictional route.

Start: Point A

Finish: Point B

Driving Directions (to a completely fictional destination):
1. Turn right onto Peachtree Street.
2. Go 5 blocks and turn left onto Wilson Boulevard
3. Take Interstate 346 N
4. Merge onto Highway 55 S
5. Take Exit 66
6. Keep right and turn right on Melrose Road
7. Your destination is at Melrose Road 2020

Right – rhymes with "bright"

Left – rhymes with "theft" (imagine your left hand getting slapped)

South – rhymes with "mouth"

North – rhymes with "back and forth"

East – rhymes with "beast"

West - rhymes with "nest"

Exit – rhymes with sit (think of your mnemonic person/object sitting down when you need to insert an exit into directions).

1. Think of a bright (bright/right) light as you approach a giant peach tree.
2. Think of a Lei placed around Woodrow Wilson's neck (Lei = Major System image for the number 5).
3. Think of a MahaRaJa (346) going back and forth (North).
4. Think of a LiLly (55) in your mouth (South).
5. Think of watching the TV show, Melrose Place (Melrose Rd) in a very bright (right) room.
6. Your destination is at house number 2020 (20 = Major System value for nose) – think of 2 noses rubbing together at your destination.

Chapter 12:
Remembering License Plates

Depending on where you live, license plate formats tend to be slightly different. Here we'll take a look at a handful.

Since the number sequence is not long, you can either use the Rhyme Method or the Major System. The Major System is much easier once you have mastered it, as it is much simpler to convert double-digit images quickly.

As far as the letters go, I personally prefer the NATO Alphabet also known as the ICAO Alphabet. It is also known as the Radiotelephony Alphabet as it is primarily used in radiotelephony communications.

It is same alphabet as is used by aviation workers and call center employees alike so that critical communications regarding number and letter combinations are clearly understood.

If you do not already know the NATO alphabet, I promise you, learning it will not be a waste of time.

Ever had to repeat your name several times to a call center agent? Trust me, it will come in handy in ways other than just for memorization.

The NATO Phonetic Alphabet /ICAO Alphabet[10]

A – Alpha	B – Bravo	C – Charlie
D – Delta	E – Echo	F – Foxtrot
G – Golf	H – Hotel	I – India
J – Juliet	K – Kilo	L – Lima
M – Mike	N – November	O – Oscar
P – Papa	Q – Quebec	R – Romeo
S – Sierra	T – Tango	U – Uniform
V – Victor	W – Whiskey	Y – Yankee
X – X-ray	Z - Zulu	

Let's take a look at a few different license plate formats. I put the Major System number to image conversions in brackets.

RT•12345

Romeo Tango 12 (Tuna) 34 (Mayor) 5 (Lei)

Image: Romeo is dancing the Tango with a Tuna and a Mayor is getting a Lei placed around his neck.

1OQCG22

1 (Tie) Oscar Quebec Charlie Golf 22 (Nun)

Image: Imagine a giant tie dragging behind a car. OSCAR (from Sesame Street, the one who lives in the trashcan) is going to QUEBEC, while CHARLIE (Charlie Brown from Snoopy) is playing GOLF with a NUN.

9JWS234

9 (bee) Juliet Whiskey 23 (gnome) 4 (row)

Image: A giant BEE is flying around you in circles. JULIET (from Romeo and Juliet) is guzzling WHISKEY while a garden GNOME is ROWing down the river.

7 BV•YD2

7 (key) Bravo Victor Yankee Delta 6 (shoe)

Image: Imagine a rustic car KEY. As you are struggling to open the door, you yell BRAVO to the VICTORious YANKEE soldier who just came back form war from a faraway river DELTA.

667 7 PN

66 (Chowchow) 77 (Cake) Papa November

IMAGE: Think of a furry CHOWCHOW dog slobbering on a CAKE next to your PAPA in NOVEMBER (say at Thanksgiving).

Safety being paramount, do not practice this while driving or crossing the road. I recommend starting with TV shows. See how many car license plates you can remember. You will be an expert in no time.

You can use the same techniques to memorize local emergency numbers. Usually they are very short, 3 digit numbers so either the rhyme or Major System will do.

Sometimes, it also pays to have the English speaking tourist police numbers memorized, they tend to be longer than the local 3-digit number for the general public so, again, the Major System comes in handy.

Another practice I have come to observe is to quickly memorize the serial numbers of large currency bills in countries that have travel warnings about currency fraud.

E.g. one country I travelled to, I was warned that a widespread scam was to take large bills from tourists, claim it was fake (they quickly swap it out with an actually fake bill) then demand another genuine bill, thereby getting paid twice and leaving you with the fake.

Chapter 13:
Memorize a Deck of Cards: Major System Practice

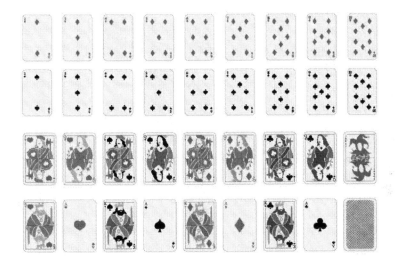

The purpose of this exercise is to reinforce the major system so you will master it for everyday use. There are a number of other ways to memorize cards if your sole purpose is to memorize only cards.

Counting cards in a casino can get you into trouble. This module is meant to be used as a memory exercise and or party trick.

One method that comes to mind is assigning celebrities and or friends/relatives to each card. For example, assign wealthy people to the Diamonds suite, people you love to Hearts, lucky people to Clubs etc.

As you progress in your memory mastery journey, you will find what works best for you as you will remember associations that are most meaningful to you.

Take the first letter from the card suit, Spades, "S", Diamonds "D", Hearts "H" and Clubs, "C" and turn it into a word, where the rest of the word corresponds to the number on the card according to the Major System.

Example. The word "Sumo", would normally convert to "03" under the Major System, however, in this exercise, we use the "S" to signal "Spades" and only take the m = 3 into account, thus "Sumo" = Spades 3.

Spades

Ace (1) – Sue**d**e
2 – Su**n**
3 - Su**m**o
4 - Sewe**r**
5 - Sea**l**
6 - Su**sh**i
7 - So**ck**
8 - Sa**f**e
9 - Soa**p**
10- Sau**ce**

Jacks - Jack the Ripper – (A spade kind of looks like a shovel, so I picked Jack the Ripper as a Jack to remember).

Queen of Spades – Mary, Queen of <u>Sc</u>otts

King of Spades – Steven King

Note: The first "S" stands for Spades.

Diamonds

Ace – (1) Diet
2 - DNA
3 - Demo
4 – Door
5 – Dalí
6 - Dish
7 - Dog
8 - Dove
9 - Dubai
10 – Dice

Jacks - Jack Daniels (Think of a Jack that is wealthy (diamonds = wealth). For me, Jack Daniels Whiskey = wealth and a global brand).

Queen – Princess Diana King – King David

Note: the first D stands for Diamonds.

Hearts

Ace (1) - Heat

2 - Hen
3 - Home
4 - Hair
5 - Halo
6 - Hooch
7 - Hook
8 - Hoof
9 - Hippo
10 – Hose

The Red H stands for Hearts.
Jack – Jack Black (Think of a Jack that you love. I absolutely love Jack Black in the movie "School of Rock".)

Queen – Hermione (from Harry Potter) on Halloween (Think of a famous female figure whom you admire/love, they don't have to be an actual queen. Helps if their name starts with the letter "H".) Other options can be Hatshepsut – Queen of Egypt, Helen Keller, Helen Mirren etc.

King – Heartbreaking King Harod

Clubs

Ace (1) - Cat
2 - Can
3 - Coma
4 - Car
5 - Cola
6 - Cash
7 - Cake
8 - Cave
9 - Cab
10 - Case

Jacks - Jackie Chan

Queen – Queen Cleopatra

King – Prince Charles

The first C in the series stands for Clubs.

Alright, now you are ready to put your knowledge into practice. We'll go line by line so it's not so overwhelming at first.

We will take the associations you leaned above and string together a story line by line. It works best if you turn into a mental image of a short film.

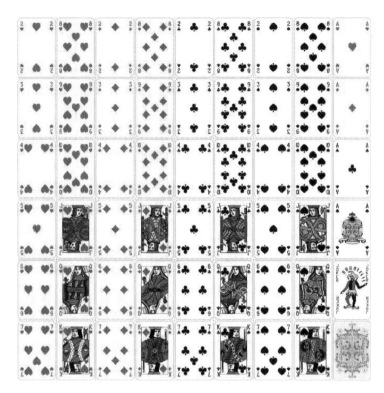

First row:

2 of Hearts - HEN
8 of Hearts - HOOF
2 of Diamonds - DNA
8 of Diamonds - DOVE
2 of Clubs - CAN
8 of Clubs - CAVE
2 of Spades - SUN
8 of Spades - SAFE
Ace (1) of Hearts – HEAT

Now let's form a (slightly absurd but memorable) story – A HEN's HOOF contains DNA of a DOVE and you can find it in a CAN in a CAVE under the SUN SAFE from the HEAT.

Now, row 2:

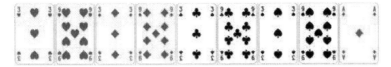

3 Hearts - HOME
9 Hearts - HIPPO
3 Diamond - DEMO
9 Diamond - DUBAI
3 Clubs - COMA
9 Clubs - CAB
Spades - SUMO
9 Spades - SOAP
Ace of Diamonds – DIET

Story for Row 2: HOME went the HIPPO to do a DEMO in DUBAI after being in a COMA from being hit by a CAB he watched SUMO, SOAPED up and went on a DIET.

Row 3:

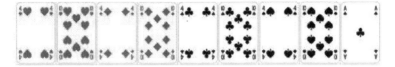

Hearts – HAIR
10 Hearts - HOSE
4 Diamond - DOOR
10 Diamond - DICE
4 **C**lubs - **C**AR
10 **C**lubs - **C**ASE
Spades - **SE**WER
10 **S**pades – **S**AUCE
Ace of **C**lubs – **C**AT

Story: A HAIRy HOSE was next to the DOOR when I took the DICE from the CAR CASE after I saved my SEWER SAUCE covered CAT.

Sound a bit odd? Yes! You have to picture it as vividly as possible. Imagine an odd-looking furry water hose next to your door. Smell the sewer, taste the sauce, feel and hear the cat purr after you rescue her from the sewer.

Let's move onto row 4:

5 of Hearts - HALO

Jack of Hearts – JACK BLACK (I ♥ Jack Black)

5 of Diamond – DALÍ

Jack of Diamond – JACK DANIELS

5 of Clubs - COLA

Jack of Clubs – JACKIE CHAN

5 of Spades - SEAL

Jack of Spades – JACK the RIPPER (because a spade looks like a shovel...)

Ace of Spades – SUEDE

Story: I see a HALO over JACK BLACK in a DALÍ paining drinking JACK DANIELS and COLA with JACKE CHAN next to a SEAL chasing JACK the RIPPER in a SUEDE jacket.

Row 5:

6 of Hearts - HOOCH
Queen of Hearts - HERMIONE
6 of Diamond - DISH
Queen of Diamond – PRINCESS DIANA
6 of Clubs - CASH
Queen of Clubs - CLEOPATRA
6 of Spades – SUSHI
Queen of Spades – MARY, QUEEN OF SCOTS

Story: There was a lot of HOOCH at HERMIONE's when we shared a DISH with PRINCESS DIANA. CASH was no problem for CLEOPATRA who hated SUSHI and invited MARY, QUEEN of SCOTTS. Then the JOKER came and ruined the party.

Final row, 6:

7 of Hearts - HOOK
King of Hearts – KING HEROD
7 of Diamond - DOG
King of Diamond – KING DAVID
7 of Clubs - CAKE
King of Clubs – PRINCE CHARLES
7 of Spades – SOCK
King of Spades – STEVEN KING

Story: Imagine a secret Santa party where, captain HOOK gave KING HEROD a DOG, who bakes KING DAVID a CAKE and PRINCE CHARLES got a very expensive SOCK with a novel knitted into it from STEVEN KING.

ALTERNATIVE METHOD: MEMORIZE CARDS USING A MEMORY PALACE

Another way to memorize cards is to take the associated word and place it in a memory palace.

For example, let's take row 5 and take your childhood home as your memory palace.

6 of Hearts - HOOCH
Queen of Hearts – HERMIONE
6 of Diamonds - DISH
Queen of Diamonds – PRINCESS DIANA
6 of Clubs - CASH
Queen of Clubs - CLEOPATRA
6 of Spades – SUSHI
Queen of Spades – MARY, QUEEN OF SCOTS

MEMORY PALACE METHOD: You drive up to the house. In the driveway there is a bottle of HOOCH. You get out of your car and HERMIONE from HARRY POTTER opens the front door. You walk into the house and you smell a delicious DISH being prepared by PRINCESS DIANA. You walk into the living room and there is CASH being thrown around the room by CLEOPATRA who wants to order food because she hates SUSHI, which was served to her by MARY, QUEEN of SCOTS. Suddenly, the JOKER enters the room and ruins the party.

I encourage you to get out a deck of cards and PRACTICE! You don't need to memorize an entire deck. Work up to it in increments of 9 cards, then string them together.

Try out both the story/string and the memory palace method. See which one works for you best.

Chapter 14:
Memorize the US Presidents

Major System Practice

A number of memory systems available use the Memory Palace System to memorize US presidents.

The reason why I prefer this system is because you can instantly recall the name and number of the president in and out of order and you are not dependent on a sequence.

There are a number of other techniques of remembering the US presidents, however, in this course, you are learning the Major System so you can apply it in all areas of your personal and professional life. Remembering the US presidents is simply a very useful exercise to reinforce using a system that will have endless applications for many years to come.

NOTE: There are a number of ways to memorize presidents using the memory palace method. The Major System takes a little bit more up front effort, but once you learn it, it has an infinite number of uses.

The Major System also allows for out of sequence memorization of items/people/events etc., while a downside of relying only on the Memory Palace method means that if you lose your place in the sequence, the rest of the sequence is lost.

Political correctness disclaimer: The more absurd you make an image in your head, the more you will remember it. None of the below mental imagery is meant to degrade any of the presidents, the imagery is descriptive of the number in the sequence, not the President per se.

Also, the image may include current celebrities to aid in recall which people are much more likely to recall than say, what an earlier president looks like.

Major System Recap:
Please complete the Major System module (Chapters 6-9) prior to this exercise.

Number	Sound	Ways to Recall	Examples
0	S, soft C, Z	Zero begins with the /z/ sound	Ice, Sauce, zero
1	T, D, TH	T and D have one vertical stroke, as the number 1.	Tie, Dye, This
2	N	The letter N has two vertical strokes.	No, Knee
3	M	The lower case letter m has three vertical strokes. The lower case m also looks like a 3 on its side.	Moo, Me, Home
4	R	Four ends with the letter "R".	Row

5	L	The Roman numeral for L is 50.	Lei, Loo, Law
6	Ch, Sh, Sch, Tsch, Cz, J, S (tissue)	The lower case letter g looks like an upside down 6. The letter J can also hold a 6 in its hook.	Shoe, Chew, Cheese, Cello, Seizure, Putsch, Giant, Jury, Schnitzel, Czech
7	K, hard C, Q, G	The letter K looks like 2 sevens linked together.	Key, Goat, Game, Cake
8	F, Ph, V	A lower case "f" resembles the number 8.	UFO, Few, View, Phone, Faux
9	P, B	A lower case p resembles the number 9 if flipped.	Bee, Pool
No value	H, Y, W, Vowels (A, E, I, O, U)	When the consonant is not pronounced, do not assign it a numerical value.	Ex. In "Law" the "w" is silent. The vowel "a" is skipped. In "Home" – the H and vowels are silent.

Example 1: A major system image for 20 is Nose. The 20th President of the United States is Garfield. I imagine the cartoon cat Garfield with a giant nose.

Example 2: The 11th President of the United States is Polk. My Major System image for 11 is Tutu, so I imagine a president in a tutu with polka dots on it.

Again, if you have not worked through your Major System images, go back and do so. It is the foundation of this program.

The goal is to come up with an image as vivid as possible to remember the presidents. The way you choose to remember them should be what's memorable to you. It can be outrageous, colorful and loud. I've chosen the best associations that have worked for me.

I'm pretty sure that James Polk never wore a tutu with Polka dots on it, but it definitely paints a vivid image so I never forget that he was the 11th President of the United States.

On the other hand, given more recent history, I associate Nixon with the Watergate scandal and have been to the Watergate Hotel in Washington DC a number of times, so I've chosen that event to associate with the major system number 37 (Mike) for it.

1. **George Washington**: (Major System 1 = **T**ie) Image: A giant TIE around the Washington Monument.

2. **John Adams**: (Major system 2 = Ho**N**ey) Someone you know named Adam, eating HONEY with honey dripping all over their Adam's apple.

3. **Thomas Jefferson**: (Major system 3 = **M**oo) Image: A cow circling the Jefferson Memorial in Washington DC while MOOing.

4. **James Madison**: (Major System 4 = **R**ow) Image: A mad son ROWing down the Potomac River in Washington DC.

5. **James Monroe** (Major System 5 = **L**ei) Image: Marilyn Monroe arriving in Hawaii with a LEI around her neck.

NOTE: Another way to reinforce Madison & Monroe is as M&Ms with Madison coming first as the letter A comes first in the alphabet.

6. **John Quincy Adams:** (Major System 6 = **Sh**oe) Image: John leading a **Q&A** session wearing giant fancy SHOEs.

   NOTE: John Qunicy Adams was the grandson of John Adams.

   I also remember him as a little kid asking for M&Ms.

7. **Andrew Jackson:** (Major System 7 = Key) Image: Michael Jackson with a KEY to the White House.

8. **Martin Van Buren:** (Major System 8 = u**F**o) Image: A van being sucked up in the air by a UFO.

9. **William Harry Harrison:** (Major System 9 = **B**ee) Image: Prince **William** and **Harry** being chased by BEEs around the White House.

10. **John Tyler:** (Major System 10 = oa**TS**) Image: Steve Tyler (of Aerosmith) eating oats for breakfast.

11. **James K. Polk**: (Major System 11 = **TuT**u) Image: A man dressed in a tutu with polka dots on it.

12. **Zachary Taylor**: (Major System 12 = **TuN**a) Image: A tailor sewing a blanket made of squishy tuna fish.

13. **Millard Filmore:** (Major System 13 = **TiM**e) Image: A president filling a sink hole with dirt while a big clock (TIME) is ticking over him and yelling at him "Fill More!"

14. **Franklin Pierce:** (Major System 14 = **D**oo**R**) Image: Pierce Brosnan as 007 busting through the White House door.

15. **James Buchanan**: (Major System 15 = **D**o**LL**) Image: A giant president doll reading a book. (Buch is book in German).

16. **Abraham Lincoln**: (Major System 16 = **D**i**SH**) Image: Lincoln balancing a dish on top of his famous tall hat.

17. **Andrew Johnson**: (Major System 17 = **ToG**a) Image: A bottle of Johnson & Johnson baby shampoo dancing around in a toga.

18. **Ulysses S. Grant**: (Major System 18 = **ToF**u) Image: Odysseus sailing in a bowl of miso soup on a boat made of tofu. Note: Ulysses is the Latinized name of Odysseus, the hero of Homer's Odyssey.

19. **Rutherford Hayes**: (Major System 19 = **TuB**) Image: A president bathing in a bathtub full of hay.

20. **James A. Garfield**: (Major System 20 = **NoS**e) Image: A president in a Garfield cartoon cat costume with a giant nose.

21. **Chester A. Arthur**: (Major System 21 = **NuT**) Image: Arthur the cartoon character eating a chest**nut**.

22. **Grover Cleveland**: (Major System 22 = **NuN**) Image: A president in a nun costume walking through Cleveland Park, a Washington DC neighborhood.

23. **Ben Harrison**: (Major System 23 = g**NoM**e) Image: George Harrison of the Beetles singing with a garden gnome.

24. **Grover Cleveland**: (Major System 24 = **NoR**way) The Nun from 2 presidents ago (who walked through Cleveland park) taking a flight to Norway.

   Note: He was president twice, before and after Harrison.

25. **William McKinley** (Major System 25 = **NaiL**) Image: A nail being driven into a bottle of McKinley tonic.

26. **Theodore Roosevelt** (Major System 26 = **NaCH**o) Image: A teddy bear eating nachos.

27. **William Howard Taft:** (Major System 27 = **NecK**) Image: Salt water taffy (the candy popular in Atlantic city) sticking to a president's neck.

28.

29. **Woodrow Wilson:** (Major System 28 = **NaV**y) Image: Wilson launching the Navy.

30. **Warren G. Harding:** (Major System **29** = **NaP**) Image: Taking a nap after a hard day's work.

31. **Calvin Coolidge** (Major System 30 = **MaZ**e) Image: Cooling off after navigating through a maze in the White House garden.

32. **Herbert Hoover** (Major System 31= **MaT**) Image: A hoover vacuum cleaner vacuuming a yoga mat.

33. **Franklin D. Roosevelt:** (Major System 32 = **MooN**) A rooster crooning at the moon.

34. **Harry S. Truman:** (Major System 33 = **MoM**) Mom reading a story about a true man.

35. **Dwight D. Eisenhower**: (Major System 34 = **MayoR**) Image: Eisenhower being greeting by the Mayor of a small town during a parade after returning home from war.

36. **John F. Kennedy**: (Major System 35 = **MaiL**) Image: Jackie O walking into the Oval Office with a hand full of presidential fan mail.

37. **Lyndon B. Johnson**: (Major System 36 = **MatCH**) Ladybird (Johnson) lighting a MATCH.

38. **Richard Nixon:** (Major System 37 = **MiK**e) Image: Giving a speech in front of the Watergate Hotel in front of a giant MIKE (microphone).

39. **Gerald Ford:** (Major System 38 = **MoV**ie) Image: A president watching a MOVIE in a Ford Focus at a drive in movie theater on the White House lawn.

40. **Jimmy Carter:** (Major System 39 = **MaP**) Image: Doing cart wheels over a giant MAP of the world.

41. **Ronald Reagan:** (Major System 40 = **RiC**e) Image: Reagan acting in a RICE commercial. Note: Reagan was an actor.

42. **George H. W. Bush:** (Major System 41 = **RaT**) Image: A large shrub eating the French dish, Ratatouille (as in the beloved Pixar produced cartoon as well as the actual dish) in the White House kitchen.

43. **Bill Clinton:** (Major System 42 = **RuN**) Image: Bill running around the White House chasing his dog, Buddy.

44. **George W Bush** (Major System 43 = **RuM**) Image: A small shrub (for Bush JR as opposed to Bush Sr. in 41) declining to drink rum at the White House.

45. **Barack Obama** (Major System 44 = **AuRoRa**) Image: Barack Obama being inaugurated President under the Northern Lights aka Aurora Borealis.

46. **Donald Trump** (Major System 45 = **RaiL**) Let's face it, I don't think anyone needs a memory system to remember this one for a long time to come, no matter which side of the aisle you are on. Let us know what mnemonic you've come up with!

Presidents recap.

Review the number and order of presidents in the previous section. Make sure you have a vivid image for each president. Make sure you see the surroundings, hear the sounds add details that will help you remember. Remember, the more absurd the image, the easier it will be to recall.

Now, who was the 11th President of the United States?

9th?
21st?
35th?
8th?
40th?
20th?
17th?
4th?

Chapter 15:
Periodic Table Mnemonics: Major System Practice

Before you start this exercise, you should have completed the Module on the Major System and have mastered the image pegs for one and two digit numbers, in order to be effective.

In order to memorize the periodic table, you will first memorize the number of the element, associate it with the major system peg that you learnt in the Major System image section, then, you will add a mnemonic that reminds you of the element.

The purpose of this exercise is to practice the Major System with meaningful numbers while enhancing general knowledge.

You do not need to be an aspiring chemist to find this exercise useful. I picked this exercise because it is far more interesting than memorizing random sections of a phone book, plus, you never know when it might come in handy for Jeopardy.

Major System Recap:

Number	Sound	Ways to Recall	Examples
0	S, soft C, Z	Zero begins with the /z/ sound	Ice, Sauce, zero
1	T, D, TH	T and D have one vertical stroke, as the number 1.	Tie, Dye, This
2	N	The letter N has two vertical strokes.	No, Knee
3	M	The lower case letter m has three vertical strokes. The lower case m also looks like a 3 on its side.	Moo, Me, Home
4	R	Four ends with the letter "R".	Row
5	L	The Roman numeral for L is 50.	Lei, Loo, Law
6	Ch, Sh, Sch, Tsch, Cz, J, S (tissue)	The lower case letter g looks like an upside down 6. The letter J can also hold a 6 in its hook.	Shoe, Chew, Cheese, Cello, Seizure, Putsch, Giant, Jury, Schnitzel, Czech
7	K, hard C, Q, G	The letter K looks like 2 sevens linked together.	Key, Goat, Game, Cake
8	F, Ph, V	A lower case "f" resembles the number 8.	UFO, Few, View, Phone, Faux
9	P, B	A lower case p resembles the number 9 if flipped.	Bee, Pool
No value	H, Y, W, Vowels (A, E, I, O, U)	When the consonant is not pronounced, do not assign it a numerical value.	Ex. In "Law" the "w" is silent. The vowel "a" is skipped. In "Home" – the H and vowels are silent.

For example: Let's take a look at the 79th element. The Major System image we picked for it was cap (c=7, p =9).

Ex. 1. The **79th** element of the periodic table is gold, thus we can remember it as a **golden cap**. Cap is the association for the number 79, and the golden color of said cap is the mnemonic hint that the element is gold.

Ex. 2. The 99th element is Einsteinium **Es** Major System Number 99 = Bib, Image: Baby Einstein wearing a bib.

Ex. 3. The 37th element is Rubidium **Rb** Major System Number 37 = **Mik**e; Major System Image: A microphone decked out with red rubies.

Ex.4. The 32nd element is Germanium **Ge** Major System Number 32 = **Mo**on; Major System Image: The Moon in Lederhosen at Oktoberfest in Germany.

Ex.5. The 90th element is Thorium **Th** Major System Number 90 = Pisa; Image: The Norse God Thor pushing against the Leaning Tower of Pisa.

You get the idea. Now let's take a look at the first 22 elements of the Periodic Table.

1. Hydrogen **H**
   Major System Number 1 = **T**ie.
   Major System Image: A fire hydrant wearing a blue **T**ie, where the blue stands for water as in part of H2O.

2. Helium **He**
   Major System Number 2 – **Knee**;
   Major System Image: Helium balloon held by a laughing girl who scraped her knee saying "hehe".

3. Lithium **Li**

Major System Number 3= **M**oo;
Major System Image: A cow holding a cell phone operated by a lithium battery and saying Moo.

4. Beryllium **Be**

Major System Number 4 = **R**ow;
Major System Image: A Berry rowing a boat.

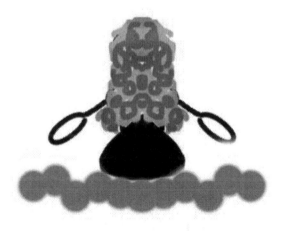

5. Boron **B**
   Major System Number 5 = **L**ei;
   Major System Image: A Lei being placed over a Bored Barron

6. Carbon **C** Major System Number 6= **Sh**oe; Major System Image: Picture of a shoe being drawn by a charcoal pencil.

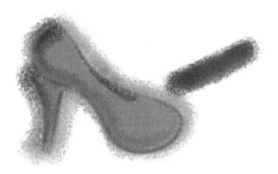

7. Nitrogen **N** Major System Number 7 = **K**ey; Major System Image: A key hanging on a dynamite keychain.

8. Oxygen **O** Major System Number 8 = **F**ox; Image: A fox with an oxygen mask on or Foxigen.

9. Fluorine **F** Major System Number 9 = **B**ee; A bee landing on fluoride toothpaste and getting stuck in it. He won't make it to bee school and will get an F on his test.

10. Neon **Ne** Major System Number 10 = Oa**ts;** Image: Oats in a neon colored bowl that's flashing in various colors.

11. Sodium **Na** Major System Number 11 = **Tut**u; Image: a soda bottle wearing a tutu, a gift from **Na**na.

12. Magnesium **Mg** Major System Number 12 = **Tun**a; Major System Image: Maggie, the Tuna fish saying that she is a magnesium rich food source but he'd prefer that you didn't eat her.

13. Aluminum **Al** Major System Number 13 = **Tim**e; Major System Image: A time machine named Al, made out of aluminum.

14. Silicon **Si** Major System Number 14 = **D**oor; Major System Image: A **si**lly pacifier being thrown against a door. (Pacifiers are made of silicone.)

15. Phosphorus **P** Major System Number 15 = **Doll**; Major System Image: A doll named **P**atty lighting a match. (Phosphorus is found in matches.)

16. Sulfur **S** Major System Number 16 = **Dish;** Major System Image: The devil serving a dish in his kitchen engulfed in a cloud and stinking of sulfur. He is wearing a shirt with the letter S on it.

17. Chlorine **Cl** Major system number 17 = **Tog**a, Major System Image A Roman named **Cl**audius in a toga jumping into a chlorinated pool.

18. Argon **Ar** Major system number 18 **Tof**u Major System Image: Katherine of Aragon eating tofu at her 18th birthday party.

19. Potassium **K** Major system number 19 = **Tub**, Major System Image: A bathtub full of kilos of posh bath salts.

20. Calcium **Ca** Major System Number 20 = **Nos**e; Major System Image: A kid from Califorina (Ca) drinking milk from a glass and dipping his nose it in. (Milk is a source of Calcium).

21. Scandium **Sc** Major system number 21 = **Not**e, Major System image = The cashier writing you a note in IKEA in Sweden (in Scandinavia).

22. Titanium **Ti** Major System number 22 = **nun**; Major System Image: A nun swimming next to the Titanic.

Chapter 16:
Geological Formations

Major System Practice Advanced Exercise

For this session of the memory exercises, I have chosen another meaningful category, geological facts.

The heights of mountains come from Wikipedia as of this writing on Feb, 2017 and are approximations.

In this exercise, we will expand the Major System references from the cards to the advanced major system matrix, which contains nouns, adjectives and verbs for each one and two digit number. Feel free to add your own.

What is important is to practice instant recall of major system values for each 1 or 2 digit number. You should practice until you can associate each 1 or 2 digit number with an image in a single second. At this point you have mastered the major system and you are ready to use it as a tool in real life without having to struggle. In time, this will become second nature.

Mount Everest
Height: 8848 m[11]
Fun Fact: Mount Everest is the highest mountain in the world and is located in the Himalayas in Nepal.
Major System Mnemonic 8848 = **Viva (88) Rough (48)**. Note, "gh" in rough make the "f" sound, therefore the major system number is "8", not "7" normally associated with the hard "g" sound.
Think of a climber having a really rough time staying alive and getting to the top of the highest mountain in the world.

Height in Feet: 29029
Major System Mnemonic 29029; 29 (___); 02 (_____); 9 (_____);

K2
Height: 8611 m[12]
Fun Fact: K2 is the second highest mountain in the world located between Pakistan and China.
Major System Mnemonic 8611 = **Fetch (86) Tutu (11)**
Think of a climber having to climb to the snow covered summit to fetch a tutu for a kid from Kindergarten class 2.

Height in Feet: 28251 Ft;
Major System Mnemonic 28251; _28 (_____); 25 (_____); 1(_____);

Mount Fuji
Height: 3776 m13
Fun Fact: Also known as "Fuji-san", and is one of Japan's sacred mountains, often climbed as part of a pilgrimage. Major System Mnemonic: **3776 = Mike (37) Cash (76)**.
Mike will need a lot of cash to climb Mount Fuji as Japan is a very expensive country.

Height in Feet: 12388 ft
Major System Mnemonic: 12388; 12 (_____); 38 (_____); 8(_____);

Mount Kilimanjaro14
Height: 5895m
Fun Fact: Mount Kilimanjaro is a dormant volcano in Tanzania.
Major System Mnemonic: 5895 = Life (58) Pool (95)
Think of yourself going on Safari in Tanzania, being amazed at the abundance of wildlife, and spotting a pool in the middle of the Serengeti.

Height in Feet: 19340ft
Major System Mnemonic 19340; 19 (_____); 34 (_____); 0 (_____);

Mont Blanc15
Height: 4808 m
Fun Fact: Mont Blanc means White Mountain and is the highest mountain in the Alps in Europe.
Major System Mnemonic: 4808 = 48 (Reef) 08 (Save)
Think of dropping an expensive Mont Blanc pen in the corral reef while diving but saving it just in time.

Height in Feet: 15761 ft
Major System Mnemonic: 15761; 15 (_____); 76 (_____); 1 (_____);

Matterhorn16
Height: 4478 m
Fun Fact: This Mountain lies between the Swiss and Italian borders. Disneyland has a large-scale replica.
Major System Mnemonic: 4478 = 44 (Aurora) 78 (coffee) Think of being in Disneyland, in front of the Matterhorn replica as the green Northern lights wash over the skies while you're drinking a cup of coffee.

Height in Feet: 14691 ft
Major System Mnemonic: 14691; 14 (_____); 69 (_____); 1 (_____);

Mount St. Helens[13]
Height: 2550 m
Fun Fact: Mt. St. Helens is an active volcano in Washington State in the Pacific Northwest of the United States.
Major System Mnemonic: 2550 = 25 (Nail); 50 (Lice)
Think of Helen hiking up a mountain, stubbing her toe on a nail and frozen lice falling from her hair.

Height in Feet: 8366 ft
Major System Mnemonic: 8366; 83 (_____);
66 (_____)

Mount Vesuvius[14]
Height: 1281 m
Fun Fact: Mt. Vesuvius is located in the Gulf of Naples and is famous for the AD 79 destruction of Pompeii.

Major System Mnemonic: 1281; 12 (Tan); 81 (Foot)
Think of walking up this volcano in the summer in Italy while your foot tans from the heat of the sun.

Height in Feet: 4202.8 ft
Major System Mnemonic: 4202.8; 42 (_____);
02 (_____); .8 (_____)

Note: In order to remember decimals, I just insert a deep, dark puddle into the story/mental picture/memory palace location.

Chapter 17:
Brain Hacks to Remember

Congratulations for getting to the end of this course! If you have read through without doing the exercises, please go back and complete them. The program works if you put in the work.

Intellectualizing the memory methods is not the same as mastering them through practice. I truly want you to succeed. I can't wait to hear your success story!

In conclusion, let's recap on how to keep your brain in tip-top shape.

- Practice Mnemonics!

In this course you have learned about making use of the Memory Palace (you born geospatial genius, you!), the Peg System (rhymes), the Shape System, the Major System and combinations of the above. Keep practicing and apply them to everyday situations. You don't need to sit at a desk and take boring tests to practice. You can do this as you are going about your day.

- o Memorize the price of produce as you walk down the aisle;
- o Memorize the name of your waiter once you order;

- o Memorize the price of the menu items you ordered;
- o Recall the name of the customer service rep on the phone;
- o Memorize your boarding time and gate as soon as your boarding pass prints;
- o Memorize the license plate of the cab or friend's car before you get in, see if you still remember when you get out.
- o Get plenty of sleep.
- **Exercise** - A highly intelligent and cultured coworker of mine once told a young guy at work that she didn't exercise because it wasn't an intellectual activity. The guy commented behind her back "well, if you don't exercise, you'll have about 10 years less of intellectual activity to do on earth". Mean? Yes, kind of.. but it's also true.

  The body is a holistic system. Your brain may have independent functions but it is not an entity independent of the body. Exercise is beneficial to the brain because it reduces insulin resistance and inflammation. Boosting mood and sleep is also a major benefit, which is a factor in improving cognitive ability.

- **Cut down on sugar and processed foods.** A diet high in sugar and processed foods is toxic to the brain[xx]. The body is a holistic system. Junk food doesn't just go to your gut.

  Common sense dictates that the toxins can spread throughout your body, including through the blood-brain barrier. Whatever can make your body sick and obese also has the potential to make your brain sick. Putting crap in your body also means putting crap in your brain.

- **Stay away from environmental toxins** as much as possible.

  It may be difficult to avoid them at the office or public places but you do control what you spray your home with. Do your research and read labels before spraying your home with anything.

- **Wash produce thoroughly!** You don't know what your fruits and vegetables were sprayed with unless you have grown it yourself.. and let's face it, many of us, myself included do not have the time to grow our own food.
- **Use Mind Maps**[xxi] – Mind Maps are a great way to unleash creativity. It is also a fab way to start on a new project, especially if you have been procrastinating or don't know where to start.
- **Doodle**[xxii] when on boring conference calls or meetings– research has shown that when your mind wanders, you don't pay attention, therefore you don't retain information. On the other hand, when you are doodling, you can still focus on what is being communicated. I tested this many, many times and it works!

Doodling keeps your mind from daydreaming, if you are drawing or coloring something, your brain can still listen intently and retain information.

By keeping your hands busy, you are essentially focusing your mind. So, if you are the boss running a meeting, give a break to those who doodle while you speak, chances are, they are paying more attention than the daydreamers.

If you are listening to an audio book or program, adult coloring books that have risen in popularity in the past few years, can actually help you retain more of the information.

- **Do yoga** to combine exercise and mediation – I am not the patient kind so the only meditation that has ever worked for me was yoga. I usually have to struggle to not fall over so naturally my mind quiets down and focuses.

Yoga helps you with breathing deeply, which can calm you down as well as gets you to focus. It can also reduce stress which is overall harmful to your body.

- **Play word games** – In today's world, when computers and smart phones are doing a whole lot of mental computing for us, we owe it to our brain to keep it in shape. We have talked about the importance of periodic recall in order to solidify long- term memories. Word games are a great way to do this.

- **Repeat and Recall** – I think it is safe to say that most of us has watched our fair share of commercials, whether on TV or online.

  I can parrot back many commercial bylines from my childhood even though I haven't heard them in many years. Repetition has a cumulative effect over time.

  This is the beauty of advertising. You may not buy right away, but you can be persuaded over time as it creates a pattern, which in turn increases familiarity. Repetition indeed helps memory although works best when combined with vivid visual imagery.

- **Make use of visualization** – As we have discussed in previous chapters, the best way to remember is to visualize using all our senses. Your brain is hit with so much information on a daily basis that in order to function, it has to ignore much of it as unimportant background noise.

  You need to choose what you want to remember, make a vivid, crazy image out of it that stands out and you will remember.

- **Create narratives** to remember. Stories are how we remember many historical and scientific concepts (think of Newton's Apple). Narratives are at the root of how we understand and communicate.[xxiii] Our minds respond to stories much better than random lists as you have learnt with the Major System and Memory Palace methods.

- **Avoid multitasking** – I used to be a proud multitasker, however, as research shows, it is not exactly a great way to be productive.[xxiv] It is so easy to get distracted by cat/dog videos, work emails, news threads, that we quickly lose focus on what we were doing in the first place.
- **Make the most of muscle memory** (aka motor learning)!

    Remember the phrase "It's like riding a bike."? You can learn so many things like:
    - Play a musical instrument
    - Learn to type faster
    - Learn Martial Arts
    - Dance
    - Create Art
- **Learn a foreign language** – Live Science[xxv] reports on a study in 2014 that was published in the journal *Frontiers in Psychology*. This study suggests that learning a foreign language helps the brain. It should be mentioned that according to this particular study, it is not yet clear whether learning a language helps memory when you are middle-aged or older.

    Having to switch between languages requires a great deal of concentration, and anything that aids concentration and attention is good for the memory, so it's likely that learning a language is a great way to boost memory recall. Studies have found being bilingual has shown to delay Alzheimer's disease symptoms by about 4 years.[xxvi]

    There is currently no cure for Alzheimer's, whenever you read a scientific study, it generally talks about delaying the onset of Alzheimer's symptoms by as much as possible. For my part, I plan on doing everything I possibly can to delay it until I'm 120 years old, by which time I don't plan to stick around.

Food is Medicine

- Why are we talking about diet in a memory book? The techniques in this program will work whether you are chowing down burgers or are eating a raw vegan diet.

However, as with sufficient sleep as well as a healthy diet, humans tend to be able to pay attention as well as work more efficiently. Eating more vegetables alone won't teach you the Major System, but it will help you feel better and concentrate more so you can pay attention to the task at hand.

I am always perplexed at how most doctors only mention eating a mostly (or fully) plant based diet as an afterthought or not at all.

- Doctors and generally people in the medical profession tend to get paid on a fee for service basis. When was the last time your doctor was financially compensated only when you got better or for preventing disease? This is a major problem with our healthcare system. We are also disease-centric instead of focusing more on prevention.

- Food is medicine but depending on what you eat, it can also be poison.

- Genetics do play a role. Humans in extreme climates such as deserts and near the Artic have evolved genetically to adhere to certain diets in order to survive.

Most people want a quick fix, a miracle pill. Even if you are from a die-hard meat eating family like I am, you can test out the benefits of a plant-based diet by starting to incorporate one plant based meal at a time. Judge for yourself and see how you feel.

- I consider myself a "cheagan" – a cheating vegan, not quite there yet but when I only eat plant-based meals, my entire day is different. There is no brain fog, which makes a very big difference when it comes to being mentally sharp and alert.

That being said, I discovered the hard way that a raw food vegan diet can have some very serious negative effects if you try to follow it in certain countries where water is contaminated so something as simple as a fresh salad can land you in the hospital for tropical diseases.

Find a balance, we already know that junk and processed foods, especially refined sugar = bad, vegetables = good. This is a course on memory techniques, not a diet plan but what you put into your body also impacts the brain.

You wouldn't buy a luxury car and fill it up with low grade fuel, would you? The same goes for your brain, it deserves the best fuel possible.

Spices

During my travels in India, I discovered the power of spices. Spices kill bacteria, which can impressively reduce the chances of you getting food poisoning.

I never got the infamous "Delhi Belly". I never once had food poisoning in India. I also never went back to eating mild food ever again. A number of studies back up the bacteria and fungus killing nature of spices. A Cornell University Study on why "some like it hot" found the following:

"Garlic, onion, allspice and oregano, for example, were found to be the best all-around bacteria killers (they kill everything), followed by thyme, cinnamon, tarragon and cumin (any of which kill up to 80 percent of bacteria). Capsicums, including chilies and other hot peppers, are in the middle of the antimicrobial pack (killing or inhibiting up to 75 percent of bacteria), while pepper of the white or black variety inhibits 25 percent of bacteria, as do ginger, anise seed, celery seed and the juices of lemons and limes."[xxvii]

Another interesting finding is that the lowest validated rates of Alzheimer's in the world are found in rural India, where a large segment of the population eats a traditional plant based diet[xxviii].

One of the best books I have ever read on nutrition is *"How Not to Die"* by Michael Greger. Brain disease kills nearly 130, 000[xxix] Americans per year and Alzheimer's kills early 85,000[xxx]. If someone close to you has suffered from the disease, you know that it is one of the most exhausting and emotionally cruel disease for both the sufferer and the caretakers.

According to Dr. Greger, a mounting evidence suggests that a healthy diet may help prevent both strokes and Alzheimer's. A number of studies suggest that a high fiber intake may keep strokes at bay. Quality fiber is concentrated in whole plant foods.

Fiber helps control cholesterol and blood sugar levels, which in turn can help reduce the artery clogging plaque in the brain's blood vessels.

Citrus is another food that has been associated with reduced stroke risk. It is also great for circulation if you have perpetually cold hands and feet. The best orange juice is the kind you make yourself. You don't need an expensive electric juicer – a $2 - $12 plastic hand juicer does the trick. That way you know with 100% certainty that you are not downing preservatives.

🟣 Antioxidants

Antioxidants are all the craze these days. They protect the body from harmful molecules called free radicals, which can cause significant damage. This damage is believed to be a factor in the development of blood vessel disease otherwise known as atherosclerosis, cancer, and other conditions.

A mentionable super-food you probably heard of is Açai, a deep purple super fruit from the Açai Palm in the Amazon that gained popularity in recent years.

During my travels to Brazil, I got hooked on the deep purple Açai shakes for breakfast and dinner. They are available on every street corner mom and pop fruit juice stand as well as shopping mall and are delicious.

Here is what acai looks like in natural and powder form:

One downside, is that it is very difficult to keep it fresh while transporting it from the Amazon and many vendors offer cheap powdered versions of it, which may be later replenished with sugar, honey and other additives.

When a new "super food" becomes popular, it becomes profitable. When it becomes profitable, low-grade impostors appear. Same goes for any supplement so take the time to research the sources you buy from.

Herbs and spices also have excellent antioxidant powers. Why not add cinnamon to your oatmeal for breakfast? According to Dr. Greger on average, plant foods contain **sixty four** times more antioxidants than animal foods.[xxxi]

Whole plant foods and spices have healing properties. While Alzheimer's has no cure, research shows that there are a number of preventative steps. While most people who suffer from Alzheimer's aren't diagnosed until their 70s[xxxii], the damage starts much earlier.

We know that what is bad for your body, it is also bad for your brain, conversely, what is good for your body, it is also good for your head.

Do you have to become vegetarian or vegan to enjoy all these benefits? As someone who used to shop at a butcher's called the "Meat with Meat, Meat Shop" with growing up, I understand the cultural implications of going vegetarian or vegan. There can be a lot of family resistance. Small steps in the right direction matter, even baby steps.

Just one whole plant meal a day will make a difference to how you feel. And who knows? Maybe in time, you will feel so much better that it will become two whole plant meals a day?

Eventually three?

The key is to start somewhere and to consciously add in healing foods and spices to our diet. You will come across a wide range of diet programs (I once went to a vegan restaurant where carrots were banned..) but one thing most agree on is that vegetables and spices are good for you.

"As the biblical passage goes: A man scatters seed on the ground... the seed sprouts and grows, though he does not know how."

Had the farmer from scripture postponed his sowing until he understood the biology of seed germination, he wouldn't have lasted very long. So why not go ahead and reap the benefits of eating fibre by eating more unprocessed plant foods?"

– Michael Greger, MD

"How Not to Die: Discover the Foods Scientifically Proven to Prevent and Reverse Disease"[xxxiii]

In Conclusion

It may take a couple readings of this book to really cement the principles of memory mastery. If you haven't completed the exercises in the book, please go back and complete them.

If you have successfully completed the exercises and mastered the techniques in the book, congratulations! You are on your way to super human memory and are ready to move onto the Advanced Memory section.

All you need is to keep applying the same principles as you go about your day. We look forward to hearing your success stories and breakthroughs!

Bibliography

[i] Pattakos, Alex, and Elaine Dundon. Prisoners of Our Thoughts: Viktor Frankl's Principles for Discovering Meaning in Life and Work. Oakland: Berrett-Koehler,, a BK Life Book, 2017. Print.

[ii] "The Pomodoro Technique.Cirillo, Francisco. " Cirillo Company. Cirillo Consulting, n.d. Web. 19 Apr. 2017. <http://www.cirillocompany.de/>.

[iii] Csikszentmihalyi, Mihaly. Flow: The Psychology of Optimal Experience. New York: Harper Perennial Modern Classics, 2009. Web.

[iv] Chia-Jung, James Rhem, and Neelima. "The VARK Modalities." VARK. N.p., n.d. Web. 08 Apr. 2017. <http://vark-learn.com/introduction-to-vark/the-vark-modalities/>.

[v] Cowan, Nelson. "What Are the Differences between Long-term, Short-term, and Working Memory?" Progress in Brain Research. U.S. National Library of Medicine, 2008. Web. 08 Apr. 2017. <https://www.ncbi.nlm.nih.gov/pmc/articles/PMC2657600/>.

[vi] "Mnemonics." Merriam-Webster. Merriam-Webster, n.d. Web. 08 Apr. 2017. <https://www.merriam-webster.com/dictionary/mnemonics>.

[vii] "Learn Hiragana, Katakana and Kanji." Dr Moku Learn Hiragana and Katakana. N.p., n.d. Web. 08 Apr. 2017. <http://www.drmoku.com/>.

[viii] Cherry, Kendra. "How Howard Gardner Developed the Theory of Multiple Intelligences." Verywell. N.p., n.d. Web. 08 Apr. 2017. <https://www.verywell.com/howard-gardner-biography-2795511>.

[ix] Mohs, Richard C. "How to Improve Your Memory." HowStuffWorks. N.p., 17 May 2007. Web. 17 Apr. 2017. <http://health.howstuffworks.com/human-body/systems/nervous-

system/how-to-improve-your-memory8.htm>.

[x] "Major System." Wikipedia. Wikimedia Foundation, 13 Dec. 2016. Web. 08 Apr. 2017. <https://en.wikipedia.org/wiki/Major_system>.

[xi] "Aimé Paris." Wikipedia. Wikimedia Foundation, 12 Apr. 2017. Web. 17 Apr. 2017. <https://en.wikipedia.org/wiki/Aim%C3%A9_Paris>.

[xii] "Major System Database." Major System Mnemonic Technique Database, List and Generator. N.p., n.d. Web. 19 Apr. 2017. <http://major-system.info/en/?n=8>.

[xiii] "Semivowel." Wikipedia. Wikimedia Foundation, 09 Apr. 2017. Web. 19 Apr. 2017. <https://en.wikipedia.org/wiki/Semivowel>.

[xiv] "Mind Mapping | Tony Buzan." Tony Buzan RSS. N.p., n.d. Web. 08 Apr. 2017. <http://www.tonybuzan.com/about/mind-mapping/>.

[xv] The Editors of Encyclopædia Britannica. "Simonides of Ceos." Encyclopædia Britannica. Encyclopædia Britannica, Inc., 14 May 2008. Web. 08 Apr. 2017. <https://www.britannica.com/biography/Simonides-of-Ceos>.

[xvi] von Restorff, Hedwig (1933). "Über die Wirkung von Bereichsbildungen im Spurenfeld" [The effects of field formation in the trace field]. Psychologische Forschung [Psychological Research] (in German). 18 (1): 299–342. doi:10.1007/BF02409636.

[xviii] Keith, Michael, and Diana Keith. Not a Wake: A Dream Embodying 's Digits Fully for 10000 Decimals. Princeton, NJ: Vinculum, 2010. Print.

[xix] Bellos, Alex. "He Ate All the Pi : Japanese Man Memorises π to 111,700 Digits." The Guardian. Guardian News and Media, 13 Mar. 2015. Web. 08 Apr. 2017. <https://www.theguardian.com/science/alexs-adventures-in-numberland/2015/mar/13/pi- day-2015-memory-memorisation-world-record-japanese-akira-haraguchi>.

[xx] N.p., n.d. Web. <http://www.health.harvard.edu/blog/nutritional-

psychiatry-your-brain- on-food-201511168626sugar+enters+blood+brain+barrier>.

xxi "Tony Buzan | Inventor of Mind Mapping." Tony Buzan RSS. N.p., n.d. Web. 08 Apr. 2017. <http://www.tonybuzan.com/>.

xxii <Nittono, Hiroshi, Michiko Fukushima, Akihiro Yano, and Hiroki Moriya. "The Power of Kawaii: Viewing Cute Images Promotes a Careful Behavior and Narrows Attentional Focus." PLOS ONE. Public Library of Science, n.d. Web. 08 Apr. 2017. <http://journals.plos.org/plosone/article?id=10.1371%2Fjournal.pone.0046362>.

xxiii Cooke, Ed. "How Story Lines Can Aid Memory." The Guardian. Guardian News and Media, 14 Jan. 2012. Web. 08 Apr. 2017. <https://www.theguardian.com/lifeandstyle/2012/jan/15/story-lines-facts>.

xxiv Pardon Our Interruption. N.p., n.d. Web. 08 Apr. 2017. <http://www.apa.org/research/action/multitask.aspx>.

xxv Wanjek, Christopher. "Learning a New Language at Any Age Helps the Brain." LiveScience. Purch, 02 June 2014. Web. 08 Apr. 2017. <http://www.livescience.com/46048-learning-new-language-brain.html>.

xxvi Craik, PhD Fergus I.M., and Ellen Bialystok PhD And. "Fergus I.M. Craik." Neurology. N.p., 09 Nov. 2010. Web. 08 Apr. 2017. <http://www.neurology.org/content/75/19/1726.short>.

xxvii Food Bacteria-spice Survey Shows Why Some Cultures like It Hot | Cornell Chronicle. N.p., n.d. Web. 07 July 2017.

xxviii PhD, V. Chandra MD, MBBS R. Pandav, PhD H.H. Dodge, PhD J.M. Johnston, PhD S.H. Belle, and S.T. DeKosky MD And. "V. Chandra." Neurology. N.p., 25 Sept. 2001. Web. 07 July 2017.

xxix Mozaffarian, Dariush, and Emelia J. Benjamin. "Heart Disease and Stroke Statistics- 2016 Update." Circulation. American Heart Association, Inc., 26 Jan. 2016. Web. 07 July 2017.

xxx Centers for Disease Control and Prevention. Deaths: final data for

2013 table 10. Number of deaths from 113 selected causes. National Vital Statistics Report 2016; 64 (2).

[xxxi] Greger, Michael, and Gene Stone. How Not to Die: Discover the Foods Scientifically Proven to Prevent and Reverse Disease. London: Pan, 2017. Print.

[xxxii] Jost, B. C., and G. T. Grossberg. "The Natural History of Alzheimer's Disease: A Brain Bank Study." Journal of the American Geriatrics Society. U.S. National Library of Medicine, Nov. 1995. Web. 07 July 2017.

[xxxiii] Greger, Michael, and Gene Stone. How Not to Die: Discover the Foods Scientifically Proven to Prevent and Reverse Disease. London: Pan, 2017.

Endnotes

[1] The word Sierra has a double "r" in it, however, as per the Major System method, it makes one sound and there fore the associated number is 04 not 044. Note that the vowels plus the consonants, x, y and w are silent in all Major System associated words.

[2] While "w" in Row is a semi-vowel, as per Major System rules, the semi-vowel "W" & consonants Y and X do not get assigned a numerical value.

[3] While "x" in the word Fox is a consonant, as per major system rules, we do not assign a numerical value to the consonants X, Y or Z.

[4] While in the word "Sierra" we convert only one "r" to its major system numerical value, in the word "Tutu", the T's make 2 separate "T" sounds, therefore we count it

[5] While there are two L's in the word Doll, as the double L only accounts for one sound, we only convert it into one number 5 instead of 55.

[6] Note that the "G" consonant is silent and the N sound is audible in the word "Gnome", therefore we only convert to numerical value the audible consonants "N" and "M".

[7] As the Major System does not convert X, Y and Z consonants to numerical values, the word "Norway" only converts the consonants N and R, resulting in the numerical value 24.

[8] Floor plans in the Superhuman System were created using Room sketcher®.

[9] To see how 395 was converted to the word MaPLe, review the Major System Recap box as well as Chapters 6 – 9.

[10] http://www.icao.int/Pages/AlphabetRadiotelephony.aspx

[11] https://en.wikipedia.org/wiki/List_of_highest_mountains_on_Earth

[12] https://en.wikipedia.org/wiki/List_of_highest_mountains_on_Earth

[13] https://en.wikipedia.org/wiki/Mount_St._Helens

[14] https://en.wikipedia.org/wiki/Mount_Vesuvius

Manufactured by Amazon.ca
Bolton, ON